How to Use This Book

Look for these special features in this book:

SIDEBARS, **CHARTS**, **GRAPHS**, and original **MAPS** expand your understanding of what's being discussed—and also make useful sources for classroom reports.

FAQs answer common **F**requently **A**sked **Q**uestions about people, places, and things.

WOW FACTORS offer "Who knew?" facts to keep you thinking.

TRAVEL GUIDE gives you tips on exploring the state—either in person or right from your chair!

PROJECT ROOM provides fun ideas for school assignments and incredible research projects. Plus, there's a guide to primary sources—what they are and how to cite them.

Please note: All statistics are as up-to-date as possible at the time of publication.

Consultants: William Loren Katz; Gary Kremer, Executive Director, The State Historical Society of Missouri; Cheryl Seeger, Missouri State Geologist

Book production by The Design Lab

Library of Congress Cataloging-in-Publication Data
Blashfield, Jean F.
 Missouri / by Jean F. Blashfield.
    p. cm.—(America the beautiful. Third series)
 Includes bibliographical references and index.
 Audience: Grades 7-8.
 ISBN-13: 978-0-531-18585-8
 ISBN-10: 0-531-18585-0
 1. Missouri—Juvenile literature. I. Title. II. Series.
 F466.3.B58 2008
 977.8—dc22   2007035320

1 2 3 4 5 6 7 8 9 10 R 18 17 16 15 14 13 12 11 10 09

AMERICA ★ THE ★ BEAUTIFUL

Missouri

BY JEAN F. BLASHFIELD

Third Series

Children's Press®
An Imprint of Scholastic Inc.
New York ★ Toronto ★ London ★ Auckland ★ Sydney
Mexico City ★ New Delhi ★ Hong Kong
Danbury, Connecticut

CONTENTS

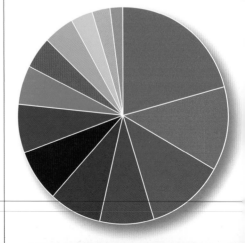

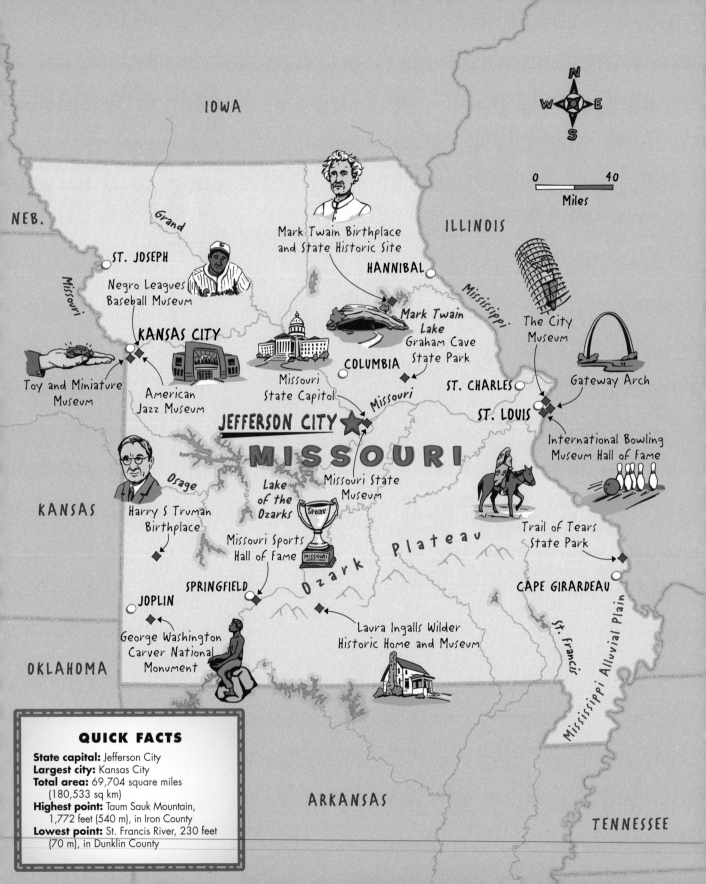

IOWA

NEB.

Grand

Missouri

ILLINOIS

N
W   E
S

0   40
Miles

Mark Twain Birthplace
and State Historic Site

ST. JOSEPH

HANNIBAL

Mississippi

Negro Leagues
Baseball Museum

Mark Twain
Lake

The City
Museum

KANSAS CITY

Graham Cave
State Park

Gateway Arch

COLUMBIA

Toy and Miniature
Museum

American
Jazz Museum

Missouri
State Capitol

ST. CHARLES

Missouri

ST. LOUIS

JEFFERSON CITY ★

International Bowling
Museum Hall of Fame

MISSOURI

Harry S Truman
Birthplace

Osage

Lake
of the
Ozarks

Missouri State
Museum

KANSAS

Missouri Sports
Hall of Fame

SPORT

MISSOURI

Ozark Plateau

Trail of Tears
State Park

JOPLIN

SPRINGFIELD

CAPE GIRARDEAU

George Washington
Carver National
Monument

Laura Ingalls Wilder
Historic Home and Museum

St. Francis

OKLAHOMA

Mississippi Alluvial Plain

ARKANSAS

QUICK FACTS

State capital: Jefferson City
Largest city: Kansas City
Total area: 69,704 square miles
  (180,533 sq km)
Highest point: Taum Sauk Mountain,
  1,772 feet (540 m), in Iron County
Lowest point: St. Francis River, 230 feet
  (70 m), in Dunklin County

TENNESSEE

Welcome to Missouri!

HOW DID MISSOURI GET ITS NAME?

The Mesquakie (also called Fox) people, who lived along the Mississippi River, had neighbors who rowed large canoes. They called them *Oumessourit*, which means "people of the big canoes." The early French explorers Jacques Marquette and Louis Jolliet tried to spell out the name they heard. Over the centuries, the European pronunciation and spelling of the Indian word changed as different explorers and settlers came into the region. The spelling became "Missouri," but even today people disagree about the pronunciation. Missourians and many southerners say "miz-UHR-uh," while Americans in other parts of the country say "miz-UHR-ee."

MISSOURI

ILLINOIS

WEST VIRGINIA

VIRGINIA

KENTUCKY

NORTH CAROLINA

TENNESSEE

SOUTH CAROLINA

8

READ ABOUT

A view of the
Meramec River
from the top of
Vilander Bluff

CHAPTER ONE

LAND

★

MISSOURI IS LOCATED NEAR THE MIDDLE OF THE UNITED STATES. So is it a western state or an eastern one? Is it northern or southern? Missouri serves as a crossroads and a borderland, connecting all of those regions. Missouri spreads across 69,704 square miles (180,533 square kilometers). Taum Sauk Mountain rises to 1,772 feet (540 meters) above sea level in the southeastern part of the state. It is Missouri's highest peak. The state's lowest point, 230 feet (70 m) along the St. Francis River, is also in the southeast.

Fishers enjoy the sunset along the Missouri River.

Eight states border Missouri, which ties with Tennessee for having the most neighboring states.

LOCATING MISSOURI

Missouri has an unusual shape, because some of its borders follow natural features. To the east, the Mississippi River defines its border with Illinois, Kentucky, and Tennessee. The southern border is with Arkansas. Most of this border is a straight line, but an area that looks like the heel of a boot, known as the Bootheel region, juts farther south. To the west are Nebraska, Kansas, and Oklahoma. The Missouri River forms the jagged northern part of this border. The northern border with Iowa is mostly another straight line.

LAND REGIONS

Missouri can be divided into four land regions. The regions' names tell you what kind of landscape to expect.

Dissected Till Plains

Great sheets of ice called **glaciers** covered the Dissected **Till** Plains at least five different times, most recently about 130,000 years ago. Thus this region, now northern Missouri, is also known as the Glacial Plains. The glaciers flattened the land, producing plains. When the last ice sheet retreated, it left gravel and soil, called till, in its wake. In Missouri, the till is about 50 to 75 feet (15 to 23 m) thick. The rivers and streams formed by water that melted off the glaciers carved up, or dissected, the plains.

WORDS TO KNOW

glaciers *slow-moving masses of ice*

till *the gravel and soil left behind after a glacier retreats*

Missouri Geo-Facts

Along with the state's geographical highlights, this chart ranks Missouri's land, water, and total area compared to all other states.

Total area; rank . . . . . 69,704 square miles (180,533 sq km); 21st
Land; rank . . . . .68,886 square miles (178,414 sq km); 18th
Water; rank . . . . 818 square miles (2,119 sq km); 34th
Inland water; rank . . . . 818 square miles (2,119 sq km); 26th
Geographic center . . . . Miller County, 20 miles (32 km) southwest of Jefferson City
Latitude . . . . .36° N to 40°35' N
Longitude . . . . 89°6' W to 95°42' W
Highest point . . . . Taum Sauk Mountain, 1,772 feet (540 m), in Iron County
Lowest point . . . . .St. Francis River, 230 feet (70 m), in Dunklin County
Largest city . . . . Kansas City
Longest river . . . . . . .Missouri River, 175 miles (282 km) in Missouri

Source: U.S. Census Bureau

Rhode Island, the nation's smallest state, would fit inside Missouri 45 times.

Onondaga Cave formations in the Ozarks

WORD TO KNOW

plateau *an elevated part of the earth with steep slopes*

The Ozark National Scenic Riverways was the first national park area created to protect a wild river system. It protects both the Current and Jacks Fork rivers, along with many caves and springs.

The Ozark Plateau

About 250 million years ago, pressure below the earth's crust thrust up the Ozark **Plateau**, an area that now lies south of the Missouri River. The Ozark Plateau was once under an ocean. For many millions of years, seashells sank to the ocean floor. They were eventually compressed into layers of limestone hundreds of feet thick. After the ocean disappeared, the limestone was on the surface. Because limestone is a soft rock, rainwater and underground springs carved many caves in it.

Parts of the Ozark Plateau are called Cave Country. Waterfalls flow among the formations in Crystal Cave near Springfield. Its walls sparkle with crystals. Marble Cave is near the Arkansas border. It includes one room in which sound carries perfectly, just as it does in the world's greatest concert halls.

As the plateau's soft rock eroded, or wore away, areas of hard rock were left behind. These raised areas that didn't erode are now the Ozark Mountains. They are among the oldest mountains in North America. Among the peaks and valleys of the Ozarks meanders the shallow Gasconade River. It is the longest (and probably most twisty) river lying completely in Missouri. It flows 265 miles (426 km) from its source in the southwest near Hartville to where it empties into the Missouri River.

The rugged St. Francois Mountains are also in the Ozark Upland. These mountains were once large volcanic craters measuring 5 to 10 miles (8 to 16 km) across. The volcanoes died out about 1.2 billion years ago. The craters slowly eroded into mountains and were covered by **sedimentary** rock. When the Ozark Plateau was uplifted, the St. Francois Mountains were also uplifted and uncovered.

The highest point in the state is Taum Sauk Mountain in the St. Francois range. Near it are the oddly named Johnson's Shut-Ins. *Shut-in* is an Ozark term for a tight gorge in a stream. The gorge forms because the bed of the stream changes from softer, more easily eroded rocks to harder rocks. The stream valley is generally wider where the soft rocks make up the streambed and becomes very narrow, or shut-in, when it passes over the hard rocks. Shut-ins have lots of sculpted rock and small waterfalls.

SEE IT HERE!

MERAMEC CAVERNS

Missouri's largest cave system is Meramec Caverns in east-central Missouri. In all, the cave system covers about 26 miles (42 km). Water moving through limestone formed the caves. Dripping water also left behind mineral deposits. Drop by drop, the minerals built up into dramatic formations. Formations that hang from cave ceilings are called stalactites. Those that rise up from the cave floor are called stalagmites. Some of the formations in Meramec Caverns look like filmy curtains. Native Americans once inhabited Meramec Caverns, as did—some say—the outlaws Frank and Jesse James.

WORD TO KNOW

sedimentary *formed from clay, sand, and gravel that settled at the bottom of a body of water*

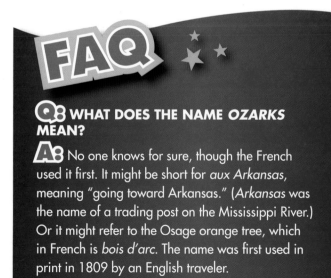

FAQ

Q: WHAT DOES THE NAME *OZARKS* MEAN?

A: No one knows for sure, though the French used it first. It might be short for *aux Arkansas,* meaning "going toward Arkansas." (*Arkansas* was the name of a trading post on the Mississippi River.) Or it might refer to the Osage orange tree, which in French is *bois d'arc.* The name was first used in print in 1809 by an English traveler.

Missouri Topography

Use the color-coded elevation chart to see on the map Missouri's high points (orange to yellow) and low points (green to dark green). Elevation is measured as the distance above or below sea level.

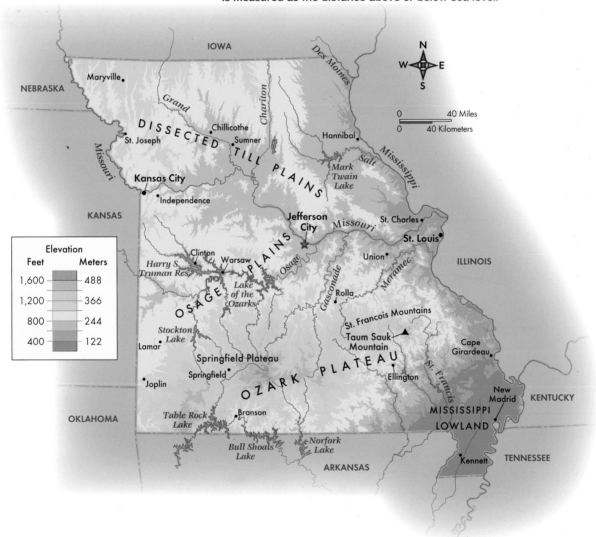

WORD TO KNOW

sediment *material eroded from rocks and deposited elsewhere by wind, water, or glaciers*

Mississippi Lowland

The Mississippi Lowland includes Missouri's Bootheel and the land just north of it. For a long time, the Mississippi River deposited **sediment** in this region when it flooded, creating fertile farmland. Pioneers

Sunrise over a Missouri cornfield

carved fields from the forests along the Mississippi and planted corn and beans there.

The New Madrid **Fault** runs through the Bootheel. Two of the strongest earthquakes in American history occurred along this break in the earth's crust in 1811 and 1812. The quakes destroyed forests and the fields of the first white settlers in the region.

WORD TO KNOW

fault *a break in the rock deep in the earth along which earthquakes may occur*

Picture Yourself . . .

in an Earthquake

It's December 16, 1811, and you're outside cutting wood on your family's farm near the town of New Madrid. Suddenly, the earth moves under your feet. What's happening? When you see a tree start to lean toward you, you dash toward an open space. But then the earth opens up beneath you! The cabin behind you trembles and then collapses. You hear a scream and run to help your brother get out from among the fallen logs. All around you, trees are crashing to the ground, their huge roots pulled up out of the earth.

You've never heard of an earthquake, but in later years you'll learn that you experienced one of the greatest earthquakes that ever rumbled through North America. It was felt westward to the Rocky Mountains and eastward to New York and Washington, D.C. The quake even changed the course of the Mississippi River, which flowed backward for a while.

VISITING THE TALLGRASS PRAIRIE

Geographer Henry Schoolcraft, exploring Missouri's prairie in 1819, wrote: "The prairies . . . are the most extensive, rich, and beautiful of any which I have ever seen west of the Mississippi river. They are covered by a coarse wild grass, which attains so great a height that it completely hides a man on horseback in riding through it. The deer and elk abound in this quarter, and the buffalo is occasionally seen in droves upon the prairies, and in the open highland woods. Along the margin of the river, and to a width of from one to two miles each way, is found a vigorous growth of forest trees, some of which attain an almost incredible size."

A herd of bison on a Missouri prairie

Osage Plains

The Osage Plains, or Osage Prairie, is a region in south-western Missouri filled with gentle hills, rolling plains, and small forests. It is on the eastern edge of the Great Plains, a vast, generally flat area that covers the central United States. Glaciers never covered the Osage Prairie, so it does not have rich till soil like northern Missouri. Tall grasses, such as big bluestem, once grew on the Osage Prairie. Today, much of the land is used to grow corn, soybeans, and hay, or to graze livestock.

THE BIG RIVERS

Only 818 square miles (2,119 sq km) of Missouri are water, yet the state is cradled by the largest river system in the United States, the Mississippi-Missouri system. The Mississippi River, which runs along the state's eastern border, is the nation's longest river. Its name means "great river." It begins in Minnesota and travels all the way to the Gulf of Mexico. The Missouri River (also called the Big Muddy) begins where several rivers join in Montana. By the time it crosses the middle of Missouri and joins the Mississippi at St. Louis, it is carrying enough water to double the flow of water in the great river.

Missouri National Park Areas

This map shows some of Missouri's national parks, monuments, preserves, and other areas protected by the National Park Service.

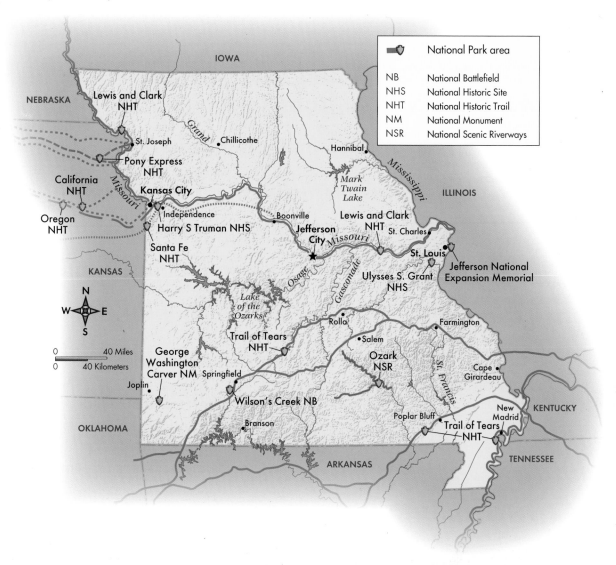

The town of Warsaw on the Lake of the Ozarks holds the records for Missouri's highest and lowest temperatures. The thermometer reached 118°F (48°C) in 1954, and dropped to −40°F (−40°C) in 1905.

Weather Report

This chart shows record temperatures (high and low) for the state, as well as average temperatures (July and January) and average annual precipitation.

Record high temperature . . . 118°F (48°C) at Clinton on July 15, 1936; at Lamar on July 18, 1936; and at Warsaw on July 14, 1954

Record low temperature . . . . −40°F (−40°C) at Warsaw on February 13, 1905

Average July temperature . . . . 79°F (26°C)

Average January temperature . . . . 27°F (−3°C)

Average yearly precipitation . . . . 37 inches (94 cm)

Source: National Climatic Data Center, NESDIS, NOAA, U.S. Department of Commerce

Q8 WHAT WAS THE WORST TORNADO IN HISTORY?

A8 The most destructive tornado in American history was the 1925 Great Tri-State Tornado. It first touched down in Ellington, Missouri, and then ripped through Illinois and Indiana. It remained on the ground for 219 miles (352 km), killing 695 people and destroying at least 10 towns and 15,000 homes.

WEATHER AND CLIMATE

Missouri has hot, humid summers. Missourians often suffer through heat waves, when the temperature tops 100 degrees Fahrenheit (38 degrees Celsius). Winters in Missouri are cold. The northern part of the state sometimes gets lots of snow, while the south gets little.

Missouri is on the eastern edge of "tornado alley." That is the area in the middle of the United States where tornadoes—nature's most violent storms—frequently occur. The state averages about 30 each year, but in 2006, Missourians experienced a record 102 twisters.

PLANT LIFE

Forests cover about one-third of Missouri. These forests are mostly in the Ozarks and along rivers. The Mark Twain National Forest is scattered in nine different sections throughout 39 counties in central and southern Missouri. Settlers and lumber companies cut its original trees—primarily oak, pine, and hickory—long ago. Much of the land was replanted in seedlings during the 1930s by the Civilian Conservation Corps, a federal

A family of black bears in a Missouri forest

agency. Today, it is a diverse landscape of heavy forest and woodlands. Violets, wild roses, columbines, and goldenrods brighten the state in spring and summer.

ANIMAL LIFE

Missouri teems with all kinds of wildlife. The Ozarks are home to many kinds of creatures, including armadillos, black bears, beavers, bobcats, coyotes, opossums, otters, muskrats, deer, raccoons, skunks, squirrels, and the occasional panther.

Many kinds of birds live on the prairie, including the bobwhite quail and greater prairie chicken. Mourning doves, ruffed grouse, wild turkeys, and American woodcocks also live in the state. At least 43 species of

ENDANGERED SPECIES

Many species in Missouri are threatened or endangered. The numbers of gray bats and Indiana bats that live in caves have dropped. The Missouri Conservation Department helps cave owners protect the bats that live within their caves.

Several endangered species make their homes in Missouri's waters. The pallid sturgeon—which is both huge, at more than 80 pounds (36 kg), and ancient (dinosaurs may have eaten it!)—swims in the Missouri and Mississippi rivers. It has been called one of the ugliest fish in North America. Not so ugly and much smaller is a tiny minnow called the Topeka shiner. It lives in prairie streams.

Wood ducks, marbled salamanders, cerulean warblers, swamp rabbits, and Ozark hellbenders are also threatened. The Ozark hellbender is a salamander that is found only in Missouri and Arkansas. Active at night, these amphibians may reach more than 2 feet (61 centimeters) in length!

A white egret and great blue heron make a stop at the Swan Lake National Wildlife Refuge.

ducks and geese are found in Missouri. Many more travel through the region along the Mississippi Flyway on their migrations. Swan Lake National Wildlife Refuge near Sumner is a popular stopping point for migrating waterfowl, especially snow geese.

Missouri's rivers are filled with fish such as bass, bluegill, paddlefish, and 15 species of whiskery catfish. The blue catfish is one of Missouri's largest fish. It can reach more than 100 pounds (45 kilograms).

PROTECTING THE ENVIRONMENT

When Europeans began to settle in the area that became Missouri, about one-third of the region was covered with prairie grasses. Today, less than 1 percent of Missouri is still prairie. As the prairies disappeared, many plants and animals that once lived there could no longer survive.

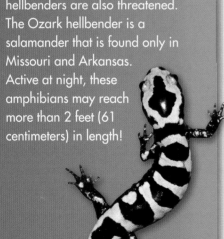

Marbled salamander

Today, Missouri's plants and animals are threatened by species that are new to the state. Many of these new species have no natural predators in Missouri, and they can easily overwhelm the local species. For example, zebra mussels, which are native to Russia, have spread throughout the region. They eat so many of the tiny plants and animals that float in the water that there is nothing left for the native mussels to eat. Silver carp, Asian carp, and rusty crayfish have also invaded Missouri's rivers. They, too, eat so much that they threaten the native fish.

Since 2005, it has been illegal to possess these creatures. The Missouri Conservation Department is working to help Missourians get rid of these species. Missourians who own land on streams and lakes are being encouraged to keep the shorelines clean so that wildlife can move along them without danger. Missouri is determined to protect its natural environment for generations to come.

A diver holds a clam infested with zebra mussels.

READ ABOUT

Prehistoric
peoples hunted
mammoths with
bows and arrows.

c. 12,000 BCE

*The first humans enter
what is now Missouri*

c. 8000 BCE

*The Dalton people
develop stone knives*

▲ c. 7000 BCE

*Archaic Indian culture
develops*

CHAPTER TWO

FIRST PEOPLE

★

THE FIRST HUMANS TO ENTER THE REGION THAT BECAME MISSOURI ARRIVED AROUND 12,000 BCE. These people, called Paleo-Indians, hunted mammoths, mastodons, and giant bison. By about 10,000 BCE, Paleo-Indians known as the Ozark Bluff Dwellers lived in caves on bluffs, or cliffs, above rivers. Over time, the climate got warmer, and the ancient animals became extinct. Life was changing in Missouri.

c. 1000 BCE ▶
Woodland culture develops

c. 1000 CE
Mississippians begin building temple mounds

1300
Native American nations form in what is now Missouri

Native American Peoples

(Before European Contact)

This map shows the general area of Native American peoples before European settlers arrived.

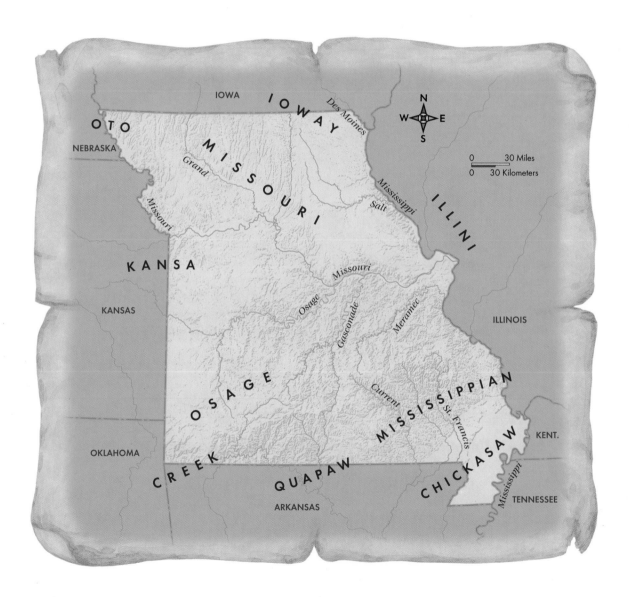

THE ANCIENT PEOPLE

After the giant mammals died out, Paleo-Indians began hunting smaller animals such as deer, squirrels, and raccoons. By perhaps 10,000 years ago, a group of Paleo-Indians called the Dalton people had developed sharp stone knives that they used to cut up deer and other animals. Their stone knives are called Dalton points.

About 9,000 years ago, the Archaic culture developed. The climate was growing warmer and drier, which meant that forests were disappearing. The Archaic Indians developed a weapon called the atlatl, which was useful for hunting in open areas rather than in the woods. An atlatl is a stick that can propel a spear faster and farther than a human arm can.

Woodland culture developed around 3,000 years ago in the eastern part of the continent. Both Paleo-Indians and Archaic people had moved from place to place as seasons changed and game migrated. Woodland people lived a more settled existence. They built round houses of wood, mud, and thatch (reeds and straw). They grew crops and made clay pottery in which they stored water, vegetables, and seeds. They also began to hunt with bows and arrows. Some of the Woodland people, called Hopewell, began to build large mounds of earth.

This Archaic culture knife blade, which dates from 8000 BCE to 6000 BCE, was discovered in Missouri.

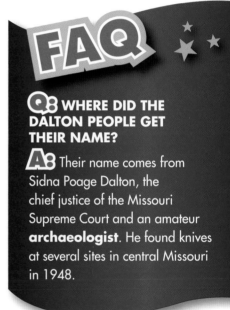

FAQ

Q8 WHERE DID THE DALTON PEOPLE GET THEIR NAME?

A8 Their name comes from Sidna Poage Dalton, the chief justice of the Missouri Supreme Court and an amateur **archaeologist**. He found knives at several sites in central Missouri in 1948.

WORD TO KNOW

archaeologist *a person who studies the remains of past human societies*

Woodland pottery

THE MOUND BUILDERS

Around 1,000 years ago, some of the people, especially in the Mississippi valley, began to build large, permanent communities. The towns were clustered around flat-topped mounds, some as tall as 10-story buildings. These people, called Mississippians, probably used the mounds both for ceremonies and as burial grounds. Some religious and political leaders lived on top of the mounds.

The largest Indian mounds north of Mexico are found at Cahokia, Illinois, just across the river from St. Louis. There are almost 70 mounds there. Missouri has its own mounds, also along the Mississippi River. The largest number is in Pemiscot County, in the Bootheel. There were once many more mounds around St. Louis, but they were destroyed as the area became more developed.

Mississippian water bottles discovered in Mississippi County, Missouri

This mural shows Mississippian women and children doing chores.

The Mississippian Indians also traded with other groups of people far away. Through this trade, they acquired copper and other goods. In 1906, some ornate and ancient copper plates were found in a Missouri field. The plates were made from copper that came from northern Michigan.

NATIVE AMERICAN NATIONS

By about 1300 CE, Native American nations began to develop. Many different peoples moved through Missouri. In the mound-building area of southeastern Missouri, Creek and Chickasaw societies developed in about 1300. The Quapaw people lived west of the Chickasaw nation, mostly in the area that became Arkansas. The neighboring Illini people (also called Illiniwek) moved back and forth across the Mississippi River in hollowed-out logs. They regarded the territory

A Mississippian face embossed in copper

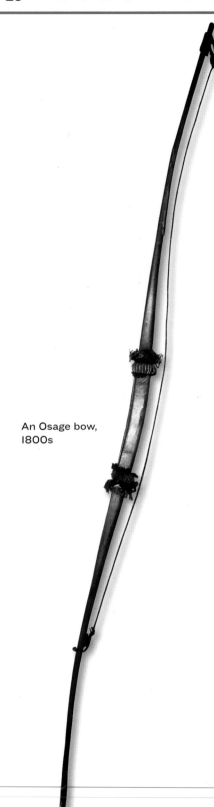

An Osage bow, 1800s

adjacent to the Mississippi River and north of Quapaw territory as theirs.

The Missouri (or Missouria) people lived in earth-covered domed houses clustered into villages. In the summer, they left their villages to hunt buffalo on the western plains. The Ioway and Oto nations were related people who held small sections of land in what is now northern Missouri.

THE OSAGE PEOPLE

The Osage nation was Missouri's largest Native American group. Osages lived in what is now the southern half of Missouri. The name *Osage* was a French mispronunciation of the group's name, *Wazhazhe*, meaning "upstream people."

Osages believed that they came to earth along the branches of a red oak tree that grew in the lowest of four worlds. Then they split into two groups, the peace people and the war people. The peace people, or Tsishu, took up farming. They were probably related to the Omaha, Ponca, Kansa, and Quapaw peoples. The war people became the Osage nation. They believed that honor stemmed from guarding their land and carrying out acts of war. Because of this, they made frequent raids into neighboring villages. They were a tall, powerful people. Many of the men stood at least 6 feet (183 cm) tall.

Osages lived in villages of longhouses. The longhouses were built of wooden poles covered with woven mats or buffalo skins. Several families lived in each longhouse. Both men and women wore clothing of deerskin.

Osages were great hunters. The men sometimes left the Ozarks to pursue bison on the nearby plains. The women tended crops, such as corn, beans, and pumpkins. They also collected fruits and nuts.

In this George Catlin painting from 1846–48, an Osage hunter pursues a buffalo.

The Osage people seasoned and preserved their food with salt. Mineral springs are common on the edges of the Ozarks, where mineral-filled water bubbles up through the limestone. As the water evaporates, salt is left behind in dried piles. These piles are called salt licks, because animals visit them to lick the salt. Osages also came to the salt licks, especially on Saline Creek (*saline* means "salty") to acquire salt.

Soon, new people would come to Missouri in search of salt, animal skins, and land. They would gradually push out the Native Americans who had long called the area home.

30

READ ABOUT

Hernando de Soto near the Mississippi River in 1541

1541

Hernando de Soto and his party become the first Europeans to enter what is now Missouri

1673 ▲

Jacques Marquette and Louis Jolliet begin exploring the Mississippi River

1715

Slaves are brought into Missouri to mine lead

CHAPTER THREE

EXPLORATION AND SETTLEMENT

★

IN 1539, SPANISH EXPLORER HERNANDO DE SOTO ARRIVED IN WHAT IS NOW FLORIDA WITH A FLEET OF 10 SHIPS. He was searching for gold. In 1541, de Soto's continued search for riches brought him and his men into what is now southeastern Missouri. De Soto, who never found the gold he sought, died soon after, and the leaderless expedition headed to Mexico. Europeans did not return to Missouri for more than a century.

1735

Ste. Genevieve becomes the first permanent European settlement in Missouri

1803 ▶

The United States buys Louisiana Territory, which includes Missouri

1820

Congress creates the Missouri Compromise

European Exploration of Missouri

The colored arrows on this map show the routes taken by explorers between 1673 and 1807.

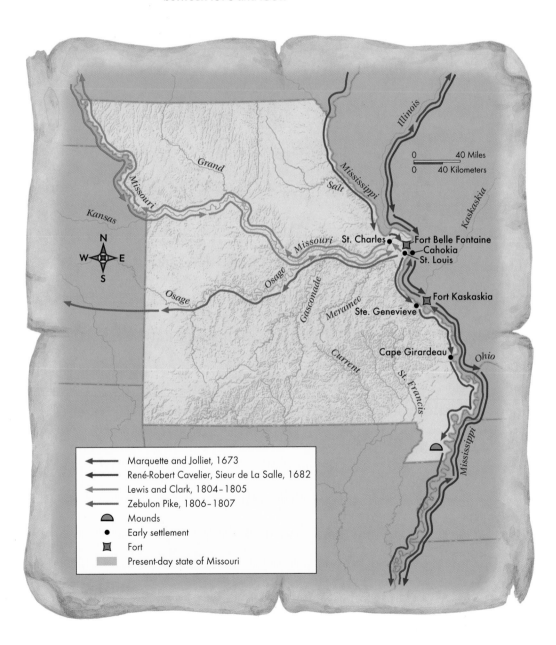

Marquette and Jolliet, 1673
René-Robert Cavelier, Sieur de La Salle, 1682
Lewis and Clark, 1804–1805
Zebulon Pike, 1806–1807
Mounds
Early settlement
Fort
Present-day state of Missouri

Jacques Marquette, Louis Jolliet, and an American Indian guide exploring the Mississippi River

THE FRENCH ARRIVE

In 1673, the French in Canada sent a priest, Father Jacques Marquette, and a young adventurer, Louis Jolliet, to explore the Mississippi valley. They traveled in canoes all the way to Missouri before returning home. A few years later, in 1682, explorer René-Robert Cavelier, Sieur de La Salle, traveled all the way down the Mississippi to the mouth of the river. He claimed the entire Mississippi River valley for France. He named it Louisiana, after the French king Louis XIV.

European fur trappers and **missionaries** soon moved into the area. The region's first-known European resident was a French priest, Father Gabriel Marest. He lived with members of the Kaskaskia nation on the west bank of the Mississippi River. Traders joined them, but they failed to build a permanent village.

WORD TO KNOW

missionaries *people who try to convert others to a religion*

STEAMBOATS ON THE RIVERS

People began using the power of steam to drive boats in 1807. The steam turned big paddles, which pushed against the water, moving the boat. Within a few years, steamboats were carrying passengers and freight along the Mississippi River at the amazing speed of 8 miles (13 km) per hour going downstream and 3 miles (5 km) per hour upstream.

The first steamboats traveled up the Mississippi to St. Louis in 1817. By 1819, they were also moving along the Missouri River. They soon became the major means of carrying cargo in Missouri. In 1860, more than 3,000 steamboats docked in St. Louis. Steamboats remained the primary means of travel on the rivers even after railroads were built in the 1850s and 1860s. They finally disappeared in the early 20th century, as their costs increased and railroads cut their prices.

A view of St. Louis in 1832

they journeyed all the way to the Pacific Ocean. They met members of 50 different Native American nations. They discovered 300 kinds of plants and animals that no European had seen before, from prairie dogs to porcupines. And they mapped much of the land. They also claimed the Pacific Northwest for the United States.

GROWING SETTLEMENTS

St. Louis was small when Lewis and Clark began their exploration. The first steamboats arrived in St. Louis in 1817, bringing more people. Many people planned to go west, but some stayed in St. Louis, providing goods and services to the people who followed them. Gradually, a great city developed.

Settlement in the Ozarks was limited for a time because the first steamboats could not travel on the winding rivers that ran through the region. Finally, smaller, more maneuverable steamboats were built. Once the ship captains learned to navigate Ozark rivers such as the Gasconade and the Osage, a new part of Missouri was opened to white settlement.

Many of the first white settlers in the Ozarks had moved there from the Appalachians. They lived by hunting and fishing. Eventually, the supply of natural food diminished, and they tried farming instead. The land was not very fertile, however. Most people could produce enough crops to feed their families but little more.

NATIVE AMERICANS ON THE MOVE

Meanwhile, Osages continued to live and hunt in the Ozarks, as they had for generations. Osages sometimes raided early French settlements in the area. But they soon learned that they could benefit if they traded with the French. Osages traded furs for guns, and for a time, the

Native Americans trading furs for weapons and other goods

Osage people prospered. But as more Europeans moved into the area, Osages were pushed off their land.

Other Native American groups were also moving into Missouri. In about 1770, some Shawnees had moved south from Ohio and settled on the Gasconade River near Cape Girardeau. They were soon joined by Delawares. Sauks and Mesquakies came into Missouri from the Great Lakes region. They had been pushed out both by the French and by the Iroquois people from farther east.

Most Native groups in what is now Missouri had supported the British during the American Revolution and the War of 1812. When that war ended in 1815, the U.S. government forced these Native Americans to give up their lands. By 1816, many Native Americans had been removed to areas west and south of Missouri Territory.

BECOMING A STATE

Year by year, more and more European Americans moved into Missouri Territory. By 1818, Missouri had a large enough population to become a state. But not all Americans wanted Missouri to be a state.

At the time, the United States was made up of an equal number of Slave States and Free States. Slavery was legal in Missouri. Some people in Congress did not want Missouri to become a state unless another state that outlawed slavery entered the Union at the same time. They wanted to retain the balance between Slave and Free States.

Finally, in 1820, Congress came up with the Missouri Compromise, which allowed Missouri to enter the Union as a Slave State at the same time that Maine was admitted as a Free State. In the agreement, Congress set Missouri's southern border at 36°30' north **latitude**. The compromise also stated that any other states formed from the Louisiana Purchase north of Missouri's southern border

MISSOURI ADDS THE BOOTHEEL

A rancher named John Hardeman Walker owned most of the Bootheel. When Missourians petitioned to become a state in 1818, the first plan left Walker's land out of the state. But he wanted to be under Missouri's laws, not those of Arkansas, which wasn't yet eligible for statehood. Congress agreed to Walker's request, and the Bootheel also became part of Missouri.

WORD TO KNOW

latitude *the position of a place, measured in degrees north or south of the equator*

Missouri: From Territory to Statehood

(1812–1821)

This map shows the original Missouri Territory and the area that became the state of Missouri in 1821.

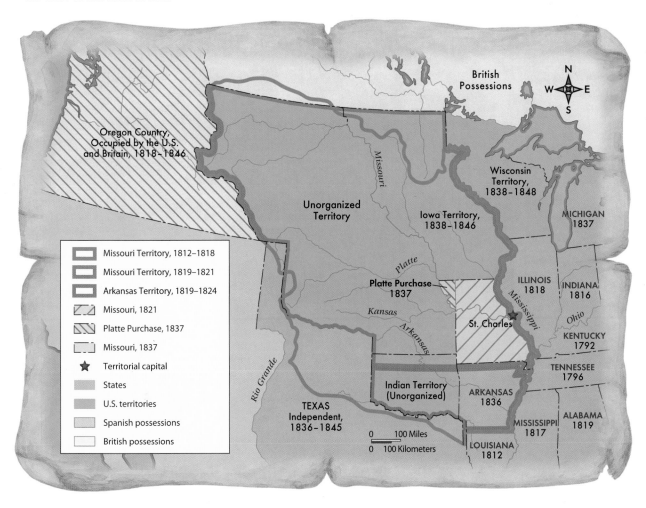

British Possessions

N
W   E
S

Oregon Country, Occupied by the U.S. and Britain, 1818–1846

Wisconsin Territory, 1838–1848

MICHIGAN 1837

Missouri

Unorganized Territory

Iowa Territory, 1838–1846

Platte

Platte Purchase 1837

ILLINOIS 1818

INDIANA 1816

Kansas

Arkansas

St. Charles

Mississippi

Ohio

KENTUCKY 1792

	Missouri Territory, 1812–1818
	Missouri Territory, 1819–1821
	Arkansas Territory, 1819–1824
	Missouri, 1821
	Platte Purchase, 1837
	Missouri, 1837
★	Territorial capital
	States
	U.S. territories
	Spanish possessions
	British possessions

Rio Grande

TEXAS Independent, 1836–1845

Indian Territory (Unorganized)

ARKANSAS 1836

TENNESSEE 1796

MISSISSIPPI 1817

ALABAMA 1819

0   100 Miles
0   100 Kilometers

LOUISIANA 1812

would be Free States. The Missouri Compromise settled the issue of slavery in the territories for a time, but the question would come back to haunt Missouri—and the entire United States.

1821 ▲

*Missouri becomes
the 24th state*

1836

*Native Americans are forced to
leave northwestern Missouri to
prepare for the Platte Purchase*

1843

*Pioneers begin leaving
Missouri along the
Oregon Trail*

GROWTH AND CHANGE

★

MISSOURI WAS ADMITTED TO THE UNION ON AUGUST 10, 1821, AS A STATE IN WHICH SLAVERY WAS LEGAL. Its central location in the United States would soon put it in the middle of the struggle over slavery. But it would also be the frontier, the starting place for adventures.

1857 ▲
The Supreme Court rules that enslaved Missourian Dred Scott has no right to sue for his freedom

1860
The Pony Express is established to carry mail from Missouri to California

1865 ▶
Missouri becomes the first slaveholding state to end slavery

Cherokees fighting the cold on the Trail of Tears in 1838

SEE IT HERE!

TRAIL OF TEARS STATE PARK

Trail of Tears State Park at Jackson is located where nine of 13 groups of Cherokees traveling the Trail of Tears crossed the Mississippi River. Winter had set in, and they had to camp on the site until the weather improved. Dozens died before they could cross the river. The park is part of the Trail of Tears National Historic Trail, a memorial to all the Indians who died along their forced journey to Indian Territory.

NATIVE AMERICAN REMOVAL

The population of the United States was growing quickly around the time Missouri became a state. Americans in the East wanted more land. In response, President Andrew Jackson signed the Indian Removal Act of 1830. This act forced Native Americans in the East to give up their land and move to Indian Territory in what is now Oklahoma.

The Cherokee nation was the largest Native American landholder in the East. Cherokees fought their removal by every means possible, but in the end, they lost. In 1838, the U.S. Army forced them on a 1,200-mile (1,900 km) journey west that is known as the Trail of Tears. For many, the trip was a death march. About one-fourth of the 15,000 Indians died along the way from hunger, cold, and disease. One of two main routes of the Trail of Tears passed through southern Missouri.

In the meantime, the Sauk and Mesquakie people from Wisconsin had been forced into the Platte River region of northwestern Missouri. The United States also moved Otoes, Missouris, Osages, Omahas, and Lakotas into that area. White settlers were supposed to keep out of the region, but they didn't. They wanted the land.

In 1836, President Andrew Jackson forced the Native people of the Platte Purchase area to give up their land. When completed the next year, the purchase added an area the size of Rhode Island and Delaware combined to the northwestern corner of Missouri. The Native Americans who lived there were soon moved to Kansas.

In 1838, the Missouri legislature passed a law making it illegal for Native Americans to live in Missouri. Rather than be forced into Indian Territory, many Native Americans gave up their traditional ways and tried to blend in with society. Missouri did not enforce the law in later years, but it was not officially **repealed** until 1909.

NEW COMMUNITIES

In 1831, Joseph Smith, the founder of the Church of Jesus Christ of Latter-day Saints (also called the Mormons), declared western Missouri the new home for his fol-

MINI-BIO

ALEXANDER McNAIR: FIRST GOVERNOR

Missouri's first governor, Alexander McNair (1775–1826) was born in Pennsylvania. He settled in St. Louis in 1804. McNair served in many posts before becoming governor, including sheriff of St. Louis County and U.S. marshal of the Missouri Territory. He was also a member of the territory's constitutional convention. In 1820, McNair was elected governor and served until 1824. He then served as an agent for the Osage people until his death.

❓ **Want to know more?** See http://history.missouristate.edu/ftmiller/LocalHistory/Bios/alexmcnair.htm

WORD TO KNOW

repealed *withdrawn; canceled*

lowers. There they would be able to live in peace. The Mormons believed that Jesus Christ would return to Earth both in Jerusalem and in Independence, Missouri.

Differences between the Mormons and their non-Mormon neighbors started almost immediately. Mormons tended to keep to themselves, and they also tended to vote for Mormon candidates. Non-Mormons feared that they would take control of western Missouri. Non-Mormons drove the Mormons first out of Jackson County and then out of Clay County. The Missouri government created Caldwell County in 1836 specifically for the Mormons. But several skirmishes followed in what is called the Mormon War. Because of the fighting, Governor Lilburn W. Boggs expelled the Mormons from Missouri entirely. His order read that the Mormons "must be exterminated or driven from the state." The Mormons settled first in Illinois before heading farther west and founding present-day Utah.

Other new communities also flourished in Missouri. In 1824, Gottfried Duden came to Missouri to look into helping other Germans immigrate. The book he wrote described Missouri in glorious terms. He said he found "beautiful nature for hundreds of miles—hills and valleys covered with trees as if an artist had created a park—your choice of climates—cheap and fertile lands." Thousands of Germans followed him to that seemingly enchanted place, founding towns such as Hermann in central Missouri. Today, Germans remain the largest ethnic group in the state.

WAGON TRAINS WEST!

When the United States took over the Louisiana Territory, Spain still ruled Mexico. Spain did not allow other countries to trade with Mexico, which at the time

Ann Hawkins Gentry was an early settler in the city of Columbia, Missouri. In 1838, she became Columbia's postmistress, a position she held until 1865. She was the second female postmaster in the country.

The town of Independence, about 1850

included the areas that are now Arizona, New Mexico, and Texas. In 1821, Mexico won its independence from Spain, and the newly independent Mexicans were eager for American goods. William Becknell, a trader from Franklin, Missouri, soon rolled into Santa Fe with a wagonload of goods.

He was soon traveling back and forth, leading wagon trains to Santa Fe. The route he followed became the Santa Fe Trail. Traders brought fabric, mirrors, and iron goods to Santa Fe and returned with furs, horses, and mules. In 1827, the town of Franklin was washed away when the Missouri River flooded. The new town of Independence was built as far west as steamboats could carry goods on the Missouri River. Enslaved Africans built most of Independence. It became the head of the Santa Fe Trail.

On May 17, 1849, most of downtown St. Louis, along with 23 steamboats docked on the river, were destroyed by fire.

FAQ

Q: WHEN WAS KANSAS CITY FOUNDED?

A: In 1821, Frenchman François Chouteau founded a fur-trading post where the Missouri and the Kansas rivers join. The trading post was destroyed by flood, but in 1833, J. C. McCoy founded the town of Westport at that same location. During the next decade, a town called Kansas was also founded in the area. In 1889, the city of Kansas became Kansas City, and in 1897, Westport became part of that city.

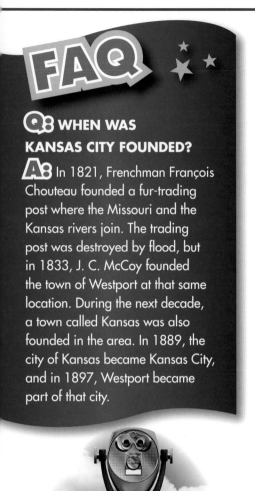

SEE IT HERE!

MISSOURI TOWN

Many people moved west from Missouri, but many people also stayed. You can see how they lived at Missouri Town 1855, located in Lee's Summit, near Kansas City. Many historic buildings, including log cabins, a tavern, and a schoolhouse, have been moved to one site. The town is so realistic that several films have been shot there.

The Oregon Trail also started in Independence. Pioneers followed this trail west to start new lives in the Oregon Country. The pioneers would gather outside Independence in April. Then they waited for the grass to grow. It had to be tall enough for their oxen or mules to graze along the route. Large numbers of pioneers first traveled the trail in 1843. In the next 25 years, more than 50,000 pioneers would make the journey.

After gold was discovered in California in 1849, other Missouri cities began competing with Independence as a jumping-off point for people heading west. Westport (which became Kansas City) and St. Joseph both boomed in the 1850s. Missouri businesspeople provided the pioneers everything they needed to travel west. They built covered wagons, they raised and sold oxen to pull the wagons, and they sold the travelers supplies for the journey, often at outrageous prices.

In the 1830s, railroad companies had begun laying track in the eastern United States. By the 1850s, railroads crisscrossed the East. The first railroad to cross Missouri was completed in 1859, but no lines crossed the Great Plains. This meant there was no easy way to get mail from the East Coast to the West Coast. Some letters destined for California were put on boats that traveled all the way around the southern tip of South America. It took months for the letters to arrive. In 1858, Congress awarded John Butterfield's stagecoach company a contract to carry mail across the continent. Butterfield's stagecoaches picked up the mail from Tipton, in central Missouri. This was the railroad's westernmost station. Butterfield could get the mail to San Francisco, California, in 25 days. In Missouri alone he had 17 relay stations where horses were changed. They were usually about 20 miles (32 km) apart.

The first Pony Express rider setting out from St. Joseph in 1860

Soon, the Pony Express was established to provide even faster mail service. On April 30, 1860, a lone rider set out from St. Joseph, Missouri, carrying U.S. mail in his saddlebags. During the coming days, that mail was transferred between 80 riders who used 420 horses stationed at 190 relay stations. The mail arrived in Sacramento, California, in just 10 days.

The Pony Express lasted only 16 months. In 1861, workers finished stringing cables for the first **transcontinental** telegraph. Now Americans with urgent messages could easily wire telegrams. Then in 1869, workers hammered in the final spike on the first railway to connect the East Coast and the West Coast. Railroads were now the fastest and easiest way to deliver mail across the continent.

WORD TO KNOW

transcontinental *crossing an entire continent*

Blanche Kelso Bruce

The first African American to serve a full term in the U.S. Senate was Blanche Kelso Bruce, who spent most of his youth in Missouri. After the Civil War, he became a wealthy farmer, and in 1874, Mississippi elected him to the U.S. Senate.

SLAVERY AND EDUCATION

After Missouri entered the Union, slaveholders from Kentucky and Tennessee became the new state's ruling class. As slaveholders became entrenched in the government, the legislature passed laws called slave codes that denied enslaved people any right to an education and tried to prevent free people of color from moving to the state.

Nuns at the St. Louis Catholic Cathedral violated the law against teaching enslaved people to read and write. They ran a secret school for slaves. One of their graduates, James M. Turner, went on to attend Oberlin College, a top school in Ohio. After the Civil War, he taught in Missouri's first public school for African Americans and was a founder of Lincoln University in Jefferson City. He eventually was appointed state superintendent of Missouri schools for African Americans.

Also violating the 1847 education law was John B. Meachum, an enslaved Virginian who purchased his freedom and moved to Missouri around 1821. Ordained as a Baptist minister, Meachum founded the First African Baptist Church of St. Louis, the first black Protestant church west of the Mississippi. He regularly helped black children learn to read and write.

TENSIONS GROW

Southerners were determined to preserve slavery in order to keep their huge profitable plantations running. Most Missouri farms were small, however, and few Missouri farmers owned more than one or two slaves. Missourians were split on the issue of slavery.

In 1854, Congress passed the Kansas-Nebraska Act. It replaced the Missouri Compromise, which banned slavery in Northern territories and allowed it in

Some Missourians moved to Kansas Territory to help turn it into a Slave State.

Southern territories. The Kansas-Nebraska Act instead gave each territory the right to decide for itself whether to allow slavery.

Many Missourians wanted the neighboring Kansas Territory to become a Slave State. Some even moved there so they could vote in favor of it becoming a Slave State. Others didn't move to Kansas, but simply crossed the border to vote, daring election officials to stop them. In 1856, a few well-armed Missourians went to the town of Lawrence, Kansas, and burned a hotel that was the center of the antislavery movement. Kansans responded by sending raiders into Missouri. The border conflict became known as Bleeding Kansas.

THE DRED SCOTT CASE

The most important slave case in American history began in St. Louis. Dred Scott had been born into slavery. In the 1830s, his master took him to Illinois and Minnesota, neither of which allowed slavery. Scott and his master returned to St. Louis in 1842. In 1846, Scott filed a lawsuit in St. Louis arguing that because he had lived in places where slavery was banned, he should be freed. Scott's legal battle lasted 11 years. Finally, in 1857, the U.S. Supreme Court ruled against him. Chief Justice Roger Taney, a Maryland slaveholder, wrote the decision. The Court said that people of African descent could not be U.S. citizens, and as a noncitizen, Scott had no right to file a lawsuit. The Court also said that the federal government did not have the power to ban slavery in the territories. Although he lost in court, abolitionists soon bought Dred Scott and his wife, Harriet. They were freed within a year.

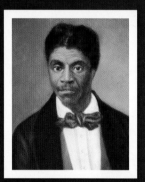

Dred Scott

The following year, the U.S. Supreme Court ruled in the case of Dred Scott, an enslaved man in St. Louis who had sued for his freedom. In its decision, the Court stated that the Missouri Compromise was not legal under the U.S. Constitution and the United States had no right to ban slavery in territories. The decision infuriated **abolitionists**.

In 1860, Abraham Lincoln was elected president. Many Southerners were convinced that Lincoln would end slavery. Not long after his election, Southern states began to secede, or withdraw, from the United States. They formed a new nation, the Confederate States of America. Lincoln was willing to fight to stop the nation from breaking apart. The country was on the verge of civil war.

MISSOURI IN THE CIVIL WAR

In Missouri, the legislature voted to hold a special convention to decide whether the state should secede. The delegates to the convention decided that Missouri should remain neutral in the war.

But Missouri governor Claiborne Jackson favored seceding. He was prepared to do all he could to swing Missouri over to the South's side. When President Lincoln called up four regiments of Missouri soldiers to fight for the Union, the governor refused to cooperate.

WOW

Only two counties in the entire South voted for Abraham Lincoln in the 1860 election, and both of them were in Missouri.

WORD TO KNOW

abolitionists *people who worked to end slavery*

The death of General Nathaniel Lyon at the Battle of Wilson's Creek

In May 1861, Jackson prepared his state military units to attack the St. Louis **Arsenal**. Nathaniel Lyon, the arsenal's commander, supported the Union. His own troops soon surrounded Jackson's soldiers and forced them to surrender. Lyon captured the capital and put a pro-Union government in place.

The first big Civil War battle in Missouri took place on August 10 near Wilson's Creek in the southwestern part of the state. Lyon was killed. He was the first general to die in the Civil War. The Confederates won the Battle of Wilson's Creek and took control of nearby Springfield. But Missouri as a whole remained under Union control. The pro-Confederate government moved to Neosho in October and set up its own legislature, which voted to secede. The Missouri Confederates later fled Neosho for Texas. Meanwhile, Hamilton R. Gamble became

WORD TO KNOW

arsenal *a place where weapons are made or stored*

During the Civil War, the U.S. Navy hired St. Louis engineer James Eads to quickly build ironclad ships—wood-framed ships covered in iron. Eads built four ironclad ships in fewer than 100 days.

the acting governor of Missouri. Through his efforts, Missouri stayed in the Union.

Early in the war, the Union cut the Confederacy in half by taking control of the Mississippi River. General Ulysses S. Grant led this effort. He would later command the entire Union army.

Later in the war, **guerrilla** raids were common in Missouri. Small bands of raiders attacked any military location they could find. Some Kansans raided Missouri, stealing slaveholders' horses and cattle and driving them into Kansas to be sold. These raiders were called Jayhawkers.

Missouri Confederate raider William Quantrill brought terror to the hearts of many. A number of teenage Missourians joined his band, including brothers named Frank and Jesse James.

To try to stop the violence, Union general Thomas Ewing arrested the wives, mothers, and sisters of known raiders. When several of the women were accidentally killed, Quantrill and his men burned Lawrence, Kansas, and killed at least 150 men and boys. Ewing responded by trying to clear the border of all pro-Confederate settlers. Their homes and crops were burned.

The war provided Missouri's enslaved men, women, and children a chance to break their chains,

WORD TO KNOW

guerrilla *describing soldiers who don't belong to regular armies; they often use surprise attacks and other uncommon battle tactics*

MINI-BIO

FRANK AND JESSE JAMES: THE TERRIBLE JAMES BOYS

Frank (1843–1915) and Jesse (1847–1882) James were both born in Kearney. As teenagers, the James boys joined William Quantrill's band of Confederate raiders and spread mayhem along the Kansas-Missouri border. After the war, the James brothers turned to robbing banks and trains. For years, they pulled off dramatic robberies across the nation. Finally, Missouri governor Thomas Crittenden offered a huge reward for the capture of Frank and Jesse. Robert Ford, a member of the James gang, shot Jesse in the head for the reward. Frank James surrendered to authorities and lived out his life on the family farm.

❓ Want to know more? See www.pbs.org/wgbh/amex/james/

AN ORDINANCE ABOLISHING SLAVERY IN MISSOURI

Be it ordained by the people of the State of Missouri in Convention assembled

That hereafter in this State there shall be neither slavery nor involuntary servitude, except in punishment of crime, whereof the party shall have been duly convicted, and all persons held to service or labor as slaves, are hereby

DECLARED FREE

This document officially ended slavery in Missouri in 1865.

About 186,000 people of color served in the Union army and helped end slavery and preserve the Union.

and many did. A young slave named Robert Hickman organized dozens of other enslaved men, women, and children to make a bold strike for freedom. They built a large raft near the Missouri River and took their families aboard. They headed east to the Mississippi and then north to freedom.

By 1864, three-quarters of all enslaved people in Missouri had fled their owners and found liberty. About 8,400 former Missouri slaves fought in the Civil War.

Missouri formally ended slavery on January 11, 1865. It was the first slaveholding state to do so. The Union won the Civil War three months later. And by the end of 1865, the 13th Amendment to the U.S. Constitution abolished slavery across the nation.

MINI-BIO

CALAMITY JANE: WILD WEST HEROINE

Calamity Jane, one of the most colorful characters of the Wild West, was born Martha Jane Cannary (1852–1903) on a farm near Princeton, Missouri. She had no schooling, but she grew up to become a great horse rider and rifle shot. In 1870, she became an army scout, and she later fought with U.S. troops against Native Americans. After traveling the West for many years, she began to appear in Wild West shows as a trick shooter. She was billed as the "heroine of a thousand thrilling adventures." She also wrote her autobiography, but there's no way of telling what parts of it were true.

? Want to know more? See www.lkwdpl.org/WIHOHIO/cana-mar.htm

REBUILDING

The raids during the Civil War had taken their toll on Missouri's farms, railroads, industries, and people. After the war, there was much to repair, buildings and relationships alike.

Missouri residents who had been enemies during the war, now had to figure out a way to work together to rebuild the state. At first, the former foes didn't work together. Some Unionists in Missouri who were in positions of power in the government at the end of the war wanted to keep former Confederate supporters out of the state government. These Unionists didn't allow some former Confederates to vote or hold public office, or to work as teachers, lawyers, or ministers. These laws were soon overturned, and rebuilding became everyone's responsibility.

BRIDGES TO THE FUTURE

Missouri's population and economy grew quickly in the years after the Civil War. Between 1860 and 1890, the state's population more than doubled. This growth was helped along by the expansion of the railroads.

In 1869, work was completed on the Hannibal Bridge. The first bridge across the Missouri River, it brought the railroad to Kansas City. The Kansas City Stockyards soon opened. Cattlemen in the West

The St. Louis Bridge, crossing the Mississippi River, opened in 1874.

could now ship their cattle to Kansas City to be sold to the highest bidder. Previously, they had to sell the cattle to the railroads, taking whatever was offered. Meatpacking became a huge industry in Kansas City, and the city boomed.

It took even longer for a bridge to be built across the Mississippi River to St. Louis. The river water there is 50 feet (15 m) deep and sits atop a thick layer of mud. But the people of St. Louis were determined to get a bridge that could carry a railroad to their city. James Eads, a self-taught engineer who had built iron-clad ships for the Union army during the Civil War, began working on the problem. He designed three steel arches that reached all the way to the bedrock beneath the mud. Eads's steel bridge—the first ever built—measured 6,442 feet (1,964 m) long. The bridge opened in 1874. St. Louis was now connected to the eastern half of the country by railroad. It was ready for greatness.

1904
St. Louis hosts the world's fair

▲ **1931**
The Lake of the Ozarks is created by Bagnell Dam

1941
The United States enters World War II

CHAPTER FIVE

MORE MODERN TIMES

★

S T. LOUIS HOSTED A HUGE WORLD'S FAIR, THE LOUISIANA PURCHASE EXPOSITION, TO CELEBRATE THE 100TH ANNIVERSARY OF THE LOUISIANA PURCHASE. More than 12 million people saw exhibits from 45 nations. Many exhibits highlighted new technologies and advancing knowledge. The people of St. Louis had shown the world that they lived in a dynamic city that embraced the future.

1945

President Harry Truman orders atomic bombs dropped on two Japanese cities

1968 ►

William Clay is elected Missouri's first African American U.S. representative

2006

St. Louis gains population for the first time in more than 50 years

Workers moving barrels along a levee in St. Louis

St. Louis hosted the Olympic Games at the time of the world's fair in 1904. It was the first time the Olympics were held in the United States.

WORD TO KNOW

levees *ridges of land built up along a riverbank to prevent flooding*

NEW LAND FOR FARMERS

At the dawn of the 20th century, Missouri was eager to use technology and know-how to improve the lives of its citizens. At that time, most of southeastern Missouri was swampland, which was often flooded by the Mississippi and smaller rivers. The counties in the region combined forces to drain the land permanently and make it productive. They built a huge system of channels to collect and drain the water off the land. Altogether, more than 840 miles (1,400 km) of ditches and 240 miles (380 km) of **levees** were built. More than a million acres of wetlands were turned into farmland.

WORLD WAR I

In 1917, the United States joined its European allies in fighting World War I. The military looked to Missouri for mules, which were used to pull cannons. Mules had been a mainstay of Missouri's economy since the days of the Santa Fe Trail. World War I also created a great demand for lead from Missouri, which was used for ammunition.

WOMEN'S RIGHTS

In the late 19th and early 20th centuries, women brought about many changes. For instance, as early as 1867, some women in Missouri began seeking the right to vote. Virginia Minor of St. Louis tried to register to vote in 1872 but was refused. She took her case all the way to the Supreme Court

JOHN PERSHING: GENERAL OF THE ARMIES

General John J. Pershing (1860–1948) was born in Laclede. As a young man, he taught in a school for African Americans and then enrolled in the U.S. Military Academy at West Point. He served with distinction in the Spanish-American War of 1898, and by 1905, he had risen to the rank of general. In World War I, he commanded all U.S. military forces. When the United States entered the war in 1917, its French and British allies, who had already been fighting for three years, wanted to divide the U.S. troops among their own units. Pershing insisted that the U.S. troops must fight together. At the war's end, Pershing was given credit for the American success in the war. He was soon promoted to the rank of General of the Armies, a rank created especially for him.

? **Want to know more?** See www.nps.gov/archive/ prsf/history/bios/pershing.htm

The St. Louis League of Women Voters' office in the 1920s

Remember - Remember
THE 23rd OF SEPTEMBER
NO REPRESENTATIO
WITHOUT REGISTRATI

FLYING SOLO

In 1919, a wealthy Frenchman offered a prize to anyone making the first nonstop flight from New York to Paris. Many people tried to win the prize, and many failed. A young pilot named Charles Lindbergh persuaded a group of St. Louis businessmen to pay for a specially designed airplane. Although the prize did not require that there be only one pilot, Lindbergh chose to fly solo. On May 20, 1927, Lindbergh took off from New York in an airplane named the *Spirit of St. Louis*. He landed safely near Paris, France, 33 hours and 30 minutes later, having traveled 3,610 miles (5,810 km). The flight made Lindbergh a hero. It also demonstrated that safe, intercontinental travel was possible, and it increased public and commercial interest in air travel.

Charles Lindbergh and the *Spirit of St. Louis*

The federal government under President Franklin Roosevelt tried to help people suffering during the Great Depression. It started programs such as the Civilian Conservation Corps (CCC), which put people to work building roads in national forests. In addition, many rural areas got electricity for the first time. Prior to this, only about 6 percent of Missouri farms had electricity.

In the 1920s, workers began building the Bagnell Dam across the Osage River, which was intended to provide electricity in the St. Louis area. When the Depression struck, jobless people came from all over the country to work on the dam. After it was finished in 1931, it formed the 129-mile-long (208 km) Lake of the Ozarks, one of the largest lakes in Missouri.

WORLD WAR II

Though such programs provided some relief, the United States did not begin to pull out of the Depression until World War II began in Europe. In 1939, Germany invaded neighboring Poland. Other European countries were soon overrun by German troops as well. France and Britain—both friends, or allies, of the United States—were fighting the Germans. Many Americans wanted the United States to stay out of the conflict. But after Japan, an ally of Germany, bombed the U.S. naval base at Pearl Harbor, Hawai'i, on December 7, 1941, the United States was at war.

When the war began, crop prices rose rapidly, helping farmers. Jobs in manufacturing multiplied, and new chemical plants opened. As men joined the armed forces, more women entered the workforce. Many got jobs making bullets, aircraft, and other wartime supplies.

Men and women building airplanes at the Curtiss-Wright Corporation in St. Louis during World War II

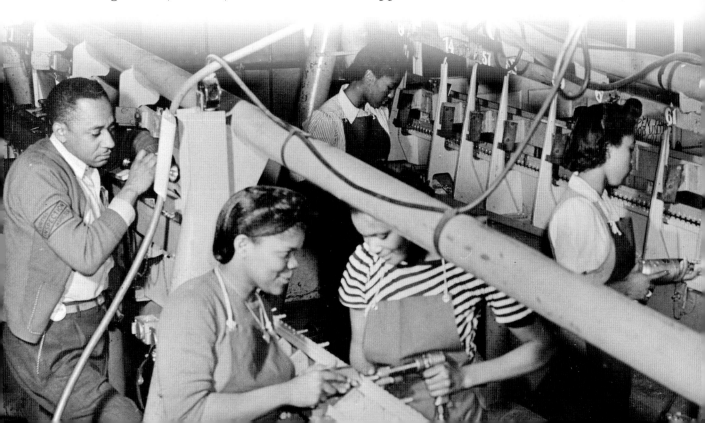

NAACP members protesting
school segregation in St. Louis

WORD TO KNOW

segregated *separated from others, according to race, class, ethnic group, religion, or other factors*

Fort Leonard Wood was established in the Ozarks in 1940 as a training camp for soldiers. Thousands of workers completed 1,600 buildings in just seven months. During World War II, more than 300,000 troops trained at Fort Leonard Wood.

In April 1945, President Roosevelt died. Vice President Harry S Truman, a Missourian, became president. In August 1945, he ordered that atomic bombs be dropped on the Japanese cities of Hiroshima and Nagasaki. The bombs leveled the cities and eventually killed more than 200,000 people. Six days after the second bomb was dropped, the Japanese surrendered. The war was over.

THE STRUGGLE FOR EQUALITY

During World War II, African Americans took on many jobs that had not been available to them before. They hoped that they would still be able to find jobs when the war ended and the white soldiers came home. After the war, African Americans from all over Missouri moved to St. Louis and Kansas City looking for work. Most ended up living in areas separate from whites.

In Missouri, white and black Americans were **segregated** in many areas. In 1896, the U.S. Supreme Court had ruled that it was legal to have separate facilities for African Americans so long as they were "equal" to facilities for white Americans. As a result, African Americans attended separate schools, rode in separate train cars, and played on separate playgrounds.

However, the facilities for African Americans were never actually equal to those for whites. In the 1930s, the National Association for the Advancement of Colored People (NAACP) began filing court cases challenging segregation laws. When the law school at the

Lloyd Gaines applied to the law school at the University of Missouri but was denied admission because of his race.

University of Missouri rejected Lloyd Gaines because he was black, the NAACP took Gaines's case to court. In 1938, the Supreme Court ordered Missouri to admit Gaines to the university or provide another school of equal stature within the state.

Slowly, segregation in Missouri broke down. In 1947, the Catholic Church ended segregation in Catholic schools. Soon thereafter, St. Louis churches stopped segregating the congregations during church services. But some white Missourians resisted the changes. In 1949, riots broke out in St. Louis when people of color were admitted to the public swimming pools and playgrounds.

In 1954, the U.S. Supreme Court ruled that segregated schools were not lawful. Missouri's African Americans hoped that this would bring about swift change, but the courts did not demand that Missouri desegregate its public schools until 1980.

In 1948, President Harry Truman ordered that the U.S. military end segregation within its ranks. Once that happened, it became more acceptable for places in the civilian world to be desegregated.

MINI-BIO

LUCILE BLUFORD: JOURNALIST AND ACTIVIST

Lucile Harris Bluford (1911–2003) grew up in Kansas City. She wanted to become a journalist, but Missouri's journalism school refused to admit her because she was African American. So instead, she enrolled at the University of Kansas. After graduating, she became an editor and publisher of the *Kansas City Call*, a black-owned newspaper. In 1939, Bluford applied to do graduate work at the University of Missouri School of Journalism. She was turned down—11 times. In 1941, the state supreme court ruled that the university must admit her. Instead, the university shut down its graduate journalism program. Almost 50 years later, the school that had rejected her awarded her an honorary doctorate.

? Want to know more? See shs.umsystem.edu/famousmissourians/journalists/bluford/bluford.shtml

Over time, African Americans in Missouri gained political power. In 1968, William Clay was elected to the U.S. Congress from a district in St. Louis. He was the state's first black congressman.

RISING TOURISM

The Ozarks were poor, rugged backcountry through most of history. The people who lived in these mountains had few ways of making a living, and they rarely visited larger towns. Then, in the 1950s, the White River was dammed in several places to prevent flooding. The last of the dams, Table Rock Dam, was completed in 1958, forming Table Rock Lake. Tourists were soon coming to the lake to enjoy the beautiful scenery.

Branson, located near Table Rock Lake, became the heart of the Ozarks' tourist industry. The town's first live show opened in 1958. Over the years, more and more theaters opened. By the 1980s, it was a center of country music, and by the early 2000s, it was attracting 8 million visitors a year.

CHANGING CITIES

Beginning in the 1960s, many white residents of St. Louis and Kansas City left the cities for the suburbs. Between 1950 and 2000, the population of St. Louis

Union Station in St. Louis

dropped from 856,796 to 348,189. People who stayed in the big cities were more likely to have low incomes. As wealthy people left, cities collected less money in taxes. The cities did not have enough money to pay for needed services. Some inner-city buildings deteriorated. Quality education also declined. Finally, state and local governments set about rebuilding inner-city areas. Neighborhoods have been spruced up, shops have opened, and new buildings have been constructed. These efforts seem to be paying off. In 2006, St. Louis gained population for the first time since 1950.

70

READ ABOUT

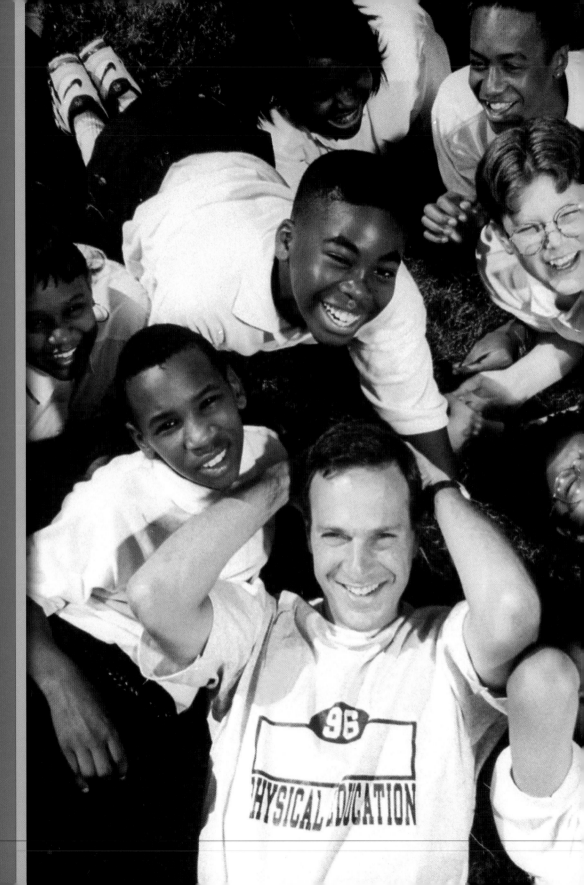

St. Louis middle
school students
and their
teacher on the
campus lawn

CHAPTER SIX

PEOPLE

★

M ANY STATES HAVE NICKNAMES THAT REFER TO THEIR BEAUTY OR TO A NATURAL RESOURCE. But not Missouri. It is called the Show-Me State. This means that Missourians aren't swayed by long words. They need to see proof. Where did this nickname come from? No one knows for certain, but one story is that Congressman Willard Duncan Vandiver delivered a speech in 1899 during which he said, "I come from a state that raises corn and cotton and cockleburs and Democrats, and frothy eloquence neither convinces nor satisfies me. I am from Missouri. You have got to show me."

People QuickFacts

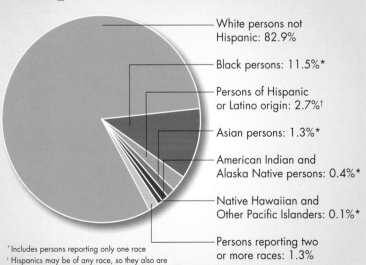

White persons not
Hispanic: 82.9%

Black persons: 11.5%*

Persons of Hispanic
or Latino origin: 2.7%†

Asian persons: 1.3%*

American Indian and
Alaska Native persons: 0.4%*

Native Hawaiian and
Other Pacific Islanders: 0.1%*

Persons reporting two
or more races: 1.3%

* Includes persons reporting only one race
† Hispanics may be of any race, so they also are
  included in applicable race categories
Source: U.S. Census Bureau, 2005 estimate

Missourians enjoying a day at
Fair Saint Louis

WHO IS A MISSOURIAN?

Missourians are northerners, southerners, easterners, and westerners. They are farmers and city dwellers. About 69 percent of Missourians live in or near cities. The two biggest cities in Missouri are Kansas City, on the western side, and St. Louis, on the eastern side, of the state.

More than four-fifths of Missourians are of European descent. The largest group, about 23 percent, traces its ancestry to Germany. The next-largest group is of Irish ancestry. Recent immigrants are more likely to be from eastern Europe. An estimated 40,000 Bosnians live in the St. Louis area. They fled a war in their homeland in eastern Europe in the 1990s.

People of Spanish descent have lived in Missouri since before it became a state. Today, about 2.7 percent of Missourians are Hispanic. Their numbers doubled between 1980 and 2000. Most of the growth was in Kansas City. Carthage, a small city in southwestern Missouri, had the most growth during that period—a whopping 2,688 percent. Many of Carthage's new

St. Patrick's Day performers in St. Louis

Participants prepare for the Hispanic Days ceremonies before a St. Louis Cardinals baseball game.

Where Missourians Live

The colors on this map indicate population density throughout the state. The darker the color, the more people live there.

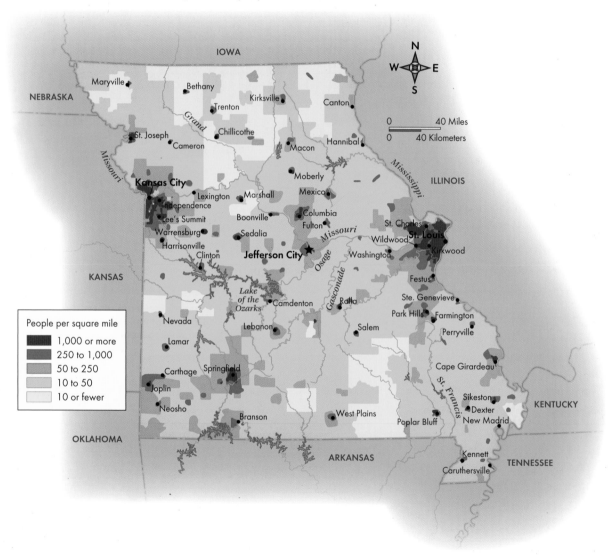

People per square mile

- 1,000 or more
- 250 to 1,000
- 50 to 250
- 10 to 50
- 10 or fewer

Hispanic residents came to work in the city's meat-processing plants. Most Hispanic Missourians are of Mexican descent. Others moved to Missouri from Puerto Rico, Cuba, and Central American nations such as El Salvador and Guatemala.

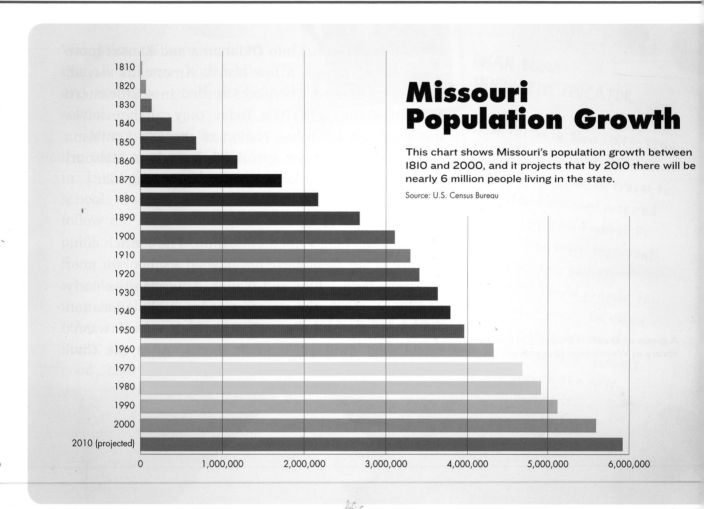

Missouri Population Growth

This chart shows Missouri's population growth between 1810 and 2000, and it projects that by 2010 there will be nearly 6 million people living in the state.

Source: U.S. Census Bureau

More than half of St. Louis's population is African American. About one-third of Kansas City's residents are people of color. Many African Americans moved to these cities from all over the country for job opportunities.

People of Asian descent make up about 1.3 percent of Missouri's population. Most are of Vietnamese or Chinese descent. Others come from Middle Eastern countries such as Afghanistan, Iran, and Iraq.

Missouri is not home to any official American Indian reservations. Native Americans were forced to

Big City Life

This list shows the population of Missouri's biggest cities.

Kansas City 447,306
St. Louis 347,181
Springfield 150,797
Independence 109,400
Columbia 94,428

Source: U.S. Census Bureau, 2006 estimate

HOW TO TALK LIKE A MISSOURIAN

Most sports fans know that Mizzou (pronounced mah-ZOO) is the University of Missouri–Columbia. But Missourians also have other unique words and phrases. Here are a few:

> *larrupin'*—great to taste
> *aim*—intend or plan
> *biggety*—stuck up
> *frog strangler*—a hard rain
> *poke*—a paper bag

HOW TO EAT LIKE A MISSOURIAN

Missouri sits at the crossroads of America, and this is reflected in the foods Missourians eat. They enjoy southern treats such as pecan pie. They also eat foods typical of the West. Beef and barbecue are popular in Kansas City, which was once the site of a major stockyard. Missouri's rivers also play a large role in how Missourians eat. Catfish is a popular catch in the state's rivers and lakes. Missourians also enjoy fresh produce from local farms.

A busy farmers' market in Kansas City

MENU

WHAT'S ON THE MENU IN MISSOURI?

★ ★ ★

Barbecued ribs

Kansas City Barbecue Sauce

Until the late 1900s, Kansas City had a thriving stockyard and many meat-processing plants. Kansas City beef was sold around the world. Today, the people of Kansas City love barbecue. They eat it at home and in almost 100 restaurants. Kansas City has its own style of barbecue sauce. It is made from a mixture of tomato, vinegar, molasses, and spices.

Ozark Pudding

Ozark pudding consists of apples and pecans, baked with just a little flour and egg to hold it together. It's great served warm with ice cream.

St. Louis Pizza

St. Louis pizza is any pizza made with Provel cheese, a white processed cheese that is popular in St. Louis. The cheese is gooey at room temperature.

TRY THIS RECIPE
Missouri Pecan Pie

Pecan farms are common across north-central Missouri. The rich, sweet nut of the pecan tree is a common ingredient in desserts, and few desserts are tastier than pecan pie. Have an adult help you with this recipe.

Ingredients:
3 eggs
¾ cup sugar
1 cup corn syrup, light or dark or mixed
1 teaspoon vanilla
¼ teaspoon salt
½ cup melted butter or margarine, cooled to room temperature
1¼ cups Missouri* pecans
1 unbaked pie shell
*If you can't find Missouri pecans, any pecans will do.

Instructions:
1. Beat the eggs until fluffy.
2. Add sugar, corn syrup, vanilla, salt, and melted butter. Mix together.
3. Spread the pecans evenly on the bottom of the pie shell.
4. Pour the egg mixture over the pecans.
5. Bake at 350°F for 30 minutes, or until the filling sets. Insert a knife into the middle of the pie. If it comes out clean, the pie is done.

Pecan pie

MINI-BIO

WALT DISNEY: ENTERTAINING YOUNG AND OLD

Walt Disney (1901–1966) was born in Chicago, Illinois, and spent part of his childhood on a farm in Marceline, Missouri, before moving to Kansas City. Though he lived in Marceline for only four years, he remembered it with great fondness and modeled Main Street, U.S.A., at Disneyland after it. Disney made his first sketches of the figure that would become Mickey Mouse while working in Kansas City. He drew actual mice that ran through his room and gradually changed them into a lovable cartoon character. Later, Disney produced a string of wildly popular animated movies and founded Disneyland, one of the world's most popular theme parks.

 Want to know more? See www.californiamuseum.org/Exhibits/Hall-of-Fame/inductees.html

Mort Walker with an actor portraying his cartoon character Beetle Bailey

ARTS AND ARTISTS

Many accomplished artists got their start in Missouri. Thomas Hart Benton (1889–1975) was the son of a Missouri congressman. He grew up mostly in Washington, D.C., and lived much of his adult life in New York City, but his vivid memories of his childhood in rural Missouri come alive in his paintings.

Cartoonist Mort Walker was a student at the University of Missouri–Columbia when he created the lazy comic-strip soldier Beetle Bailey around 1950. Beetle has been appearing in the funny pages ever since. Today, a life-size bronze statue of Beetle Bailey is on the university campus. Walker is also the creator of the cartoon *Hi and Lois* about life in a suburban family.

Artist Rose O'Neill's family moved from Pennsylvania to the Ozarks, near Branson. She designed a cute figure that she thought looked like Cupid, so she called it the Kewpie doll. First appearing in 1910, Kewpie dolls quickly became popular in the United States and Europe.

In recent decades, the Ozarks have become a popular tourist destination. This has helped revive the craft of wood carving, which had almost died out. Peter Engler played a large role in that revival. In 1962, he opened a wood-carving shop in Branson, where he specialized in making traditional Santa Claus figures. Many other wood-carvers have also set up shop in Branson.

MINI-BIO

SCOTT JOPLIN: KING OF RAGTIME

Scott Joplin (c. 1867–1917) was born in Texas and began playing piano as a young child. He eventually settled in Sedalia, where he studied music at George R. Smith College. In the 1890s, he developed the style that became ragtime. In 1899, he wrote "Maple Leaf Rag"—named for an African American social club in Sedalia—and it was a huge success. This encouraged him to move to St. Louis, where he wrote masterpieces such as "The Entertainer," which was used as the theme song for the movie The Sting, and "Ragtime Dance." In 1976, long after his death, Joplin was awarded a Pulitzer Prize for his contributions to American music.

❓ **Want to know more?** See www.scottjoplin.org/biography.htm

MUSICIANS

Missouri has long been a center of musical innovation. Ragtime, perhaps the first type of music invented in the United States, was popular in the late 19th and early 20th centuries. Ragtime stresses musical notes between the regular beats, called syncopation, which is common in traditional African music. Scott Joplin, a pianist and composer from Sedalia, was the "King of Ragtime."

Around the same time, jazz was also developing. Kansas City was an early center for jazz. Like ragtime, jazz uses syncopation, but it also uses improvisation. Performers make up some of the music as they go along.

First one musician solos, and then another, almost as if they are having a conversation.

Charlie "Bird" Parker, Coleman Hawkins, Fletcher Henderson, Count Basie, and Mary Lou Williams were Kansas City jazz favorites starting in the 1930s. Their style, which is relaxed and uses complicated improvisations, became known as Kansas City jazz. St. Louis singer Josephine Baker performed many kinds of music, including jazz. After moving to Paris, France, in 1925, she became one of the biggest stars in Europe.

Rap artist Nelly is from St. Louis.

MINI-BIO

JOSEPHINE BAKER: ENTERTAINER AND ACTIVIST

Josephine Baker (1906–1975) began her career dancing in the streets of her hometown of St. Louis when she was a child. By the time she was a teenager, she was performing in Broadway musicals in New York. Her popularity took her to Paris, France, where she became a top dancer in Paris nightclubs. In 1927, she earned more money than any other entertainer in Europe. Returning often to the United States, she actively supported the struggle for equality and refused to appear before segregated audiences. When she died in Paris in 1975, 20,000 people turned out for her funeral procession.

? **Want to know more?** See stlouiswalkoffame.org/inductees/josephine-baker.html

Musician Sheryl Crow grew up in Kennett.

MINI-BIO

MARK TWAIN: NOVELIST

Mark Twain (1835–1910), one of the country's greatest novelists, was born Samuel Clemens in Florida, Missouri. He grew up in Hannibal, which was a slave-trading center. Twain's father owned slaves, and young Sam never forgot seeing his father sell a slave away "from his home, his mother, and his friends." Twain once wrote, "Slavery was maintained by the lie of silent assertion—the silent assertion that there wasn't anything going on in which humane and intelligent people were interested." Twain placed Jim, an enslaved boy desperately running to freedom, at the center of his classic novel *The Adventures of Huckleberry Finn*. Throughout his life, Twain denounced oppression of all kinds.

? Want to know more? See www.pbs.org/marktwain/

More recently, Missouri has produced musicians who work in many different styles. Nelly, who grew up as Cornell Haynes Jr. in St. Louis, is one of the best-selling rap singers of all time. Sheryl Crow, an award-winning singer and songwriter, grew up in Kennett, in southeastern Missouri.

WRITERS

No writer is more closely associated with Missouri than the humorist-novelist Mark Twain. He used his Missouri childhood in his classic novels *The Adventures of Tom Sawyer* and *The Adventures of Huckleberry Finn*.

WORD TO KNOW

feminist *holding the belief that women are the political, economic, and social equals of men*

St. Louis-born Kate Chopin wrote *The Awakening,* an early **feminist** novel about a woman who is trapped by her role as wife and mother. Born in Columbus, Mississippi, playwright Tennessee Williams and his family moved to St. Louis when he was seven. He set his play *The Glass Menagerie,* about a young man trying to deal with his controlling mother and his desperately shy sister, in that city. Williams eventually won two Pulitzer Prizes, first for *The Glass Menagerie* and then for *Cat on a Hot Tin Roof.* Maya Angelou recounted her rough St. Louis childhood in books such as *I Know Why the Caged Bird Sings.* Children's writer Laura Ingalls Wilder also drew on her own childhood when writing her beloved Little House series.

Joseph Pulitzer founded the *St. Louis Post-Dispatch,* the biggest newspaper in Missouri. In his will, Pulitzer

Playwright Tennessee Williams writing at his desk in 1948

MAYA ANGELOU: POET AND NOVELIST

Maya Angelou (1928–) was named Marguerite Johnson when she was born in St. Louis. After her parents divorced, she moved frequently, living sometimes with her grandmother in Arkansas and sometimes with her mother in Missouri or California. Beginning at age eight, Angelou refused to speak for five years because she thought her words had caused a man to be murdered. She later became a singer, actor, dancer, newspaper editor, poet, and civil rights worker. Her complicated life has provided the material for six autobiographical novels, including *I Know Why the Caged Bird Sings* and *All God's Children Need Traveling Shoes.*

❓ **Want to know more?** See www.poets.org/poet.php/prmPID/87

Journalist and publisher Joseph Pulitzer

established prizes for outstanding journalism and literary writing. The first Pulitzer Prizes were awarded in 1917. Prizes were later added in other fields such as music.

Missouri has also produced many innovative poets. T. S. Eliot, who grew up in a prominent St. Louis family, was a giant of modern poetry. His long poem *The Waste Land,* published in 1922, expressed the frustration and restlessness felt by many young people at the time. Eliot received the Nobel Prize in Literature, the world's highest literary honor, in 1948. Mona Van Duyn, a longtime teacher at Washington University in St. Louis, became the first female U.S. poet laureate in 1992. Another Missouri poet, Marianne Moore, used precise language to describe images from nature.

MISSOURI SPORTS

Missourians are crazy about sports. Football fans cheer on the St. Louis Rams and the Kansas City Chiefs, hockey fans thrill to the slapshots of the St. Louis Blues, while soccer fans root for the Kansas City Wizards.

The St. Louis Cardinals are the state's oldest professional sports team. They have been around since 1882, when they were called the St. Louis Brown Stockings. Unlike most Major League Baseball teams,

Members of the Kansas City Wizards soccer team celebrate a goal against the Colorado Rapids.

Fans taking in a St. Louis Cardinals game

the Cardinals have remained in the same city throughout their history. As of 2008, the Cards had won the World Series 10 times, more than any other team except the New York Yankees.

In Kansas City, baseball fans root for the Royals. In 1985, Missourians were thrilled when the Royals faced the Cardinals in the World Series. The two top teams in baseball were both from the Show-Me State.

MINI-BIO

ROBERT "CAL" HUBBARD: DOUBLE HALL OF FAMER

The only person ever inducted into both the National Football League Hall of Fame (1963) and the Major League Baseball Hall of Fame (1973) was Missouri's Robert "Cal" Hubbard (1900–1977). Playing for the New York Giants and then the Green Bay Packers football teams, he invented the position of linebacker. While playing football, he also umpired minor league baseball games. After retiring from football, he became a major league umpire and worked many World Series games.

Want to know more? See www.profootballhof.com/hof/member.jsp?player_id=101

CHAPTER SEVEN

GOVERNMENT

★

THE MISSOURI STATE GOVERN-
MENT, CONVINCED THAT EVERY
CHILD IS "BORN TO LEARN,"
BEGAN A PROGRAM CALLED PARENTS AS
TEACHERS IN 1981. It helps organizations
identify children who might need extra help
before they get to kindergarten and then
teaches parents how to help their children
learn. Families can take part when their children are as young as six months old. Parents
as Teachers is now a successful national orga-
nization, but it all began with the work of the
Missouri government and the local schools.

THINK ABOUT IT!

Combining City and Suburb

Some people in the St. Louis area have considered the idea of merging the city of St. Louis with St. Louis County to become one big city. If that happened, St. Louis would be the nation's sixth-largest city.

Why do it? Because the social and economic problems St. Louis faces don't stop at the city limits. Issues related to jobs, transportation, education, and crime affect both city and suburbs, so the local governments may be more effective at solving problems if they work on them as one entity. One area where the merger may help is education. In 2007, the city's public schools were taken over by the state because they were performing so poorly. Many people believe a merger would provide city schools with additional funds and resources.

Some people in the suburbs are opposed to the merger because they are afraid it would raise their taxes. One writer, talking to people in the suburbs, argued, "There are a million reasons why [the separation of city and suburb] is bad for the residents of St. Louis, but it is also bad for you. If you were part of St. Louis, it would only take a very, very small portion of your money to solve what is a very bad problem. And it's not like it's someone else's problem. It's your problem, because it's just right across the freeway and social problems don't respect city lines."

JUDICIAL BRANCH

The judicial branch consists of the state's court system. The court system has three levels: circuit courts, the court of appeals, and the supreme court. Most trials are held in Missouri's 45 circuit courts. Someone who believes a circuit court made a mistake can ask the Missouri Court of Appeals to review the case. The state has three appeals courts, in St. Louis, Kansas City, and Springfield. The Missouri Supreme Court reviews decisions of the appeals courts. It also hears any cases involving the state constitution, the death penalty, or U.S. treaties. The governor appoints the supreme court's seven judges, but each judge must be approved by a vote of the people after one year in office. The judges serve 12-year terms.

LOCAL GOVERNMENT

Missouri is divided into 114 counties and the city of St. Louis. There is also a county of St. Louis, but the city is not part of it. St. Louis County is the state's largest county by population. The smallest county by both size and population is Worth County in the northwest. It has difficulty

Missouri Counties

This map shows the 114 counties in Missouri, plus the independent city of St. Louis. Jefferson City, the state capital, is indicated with a star.

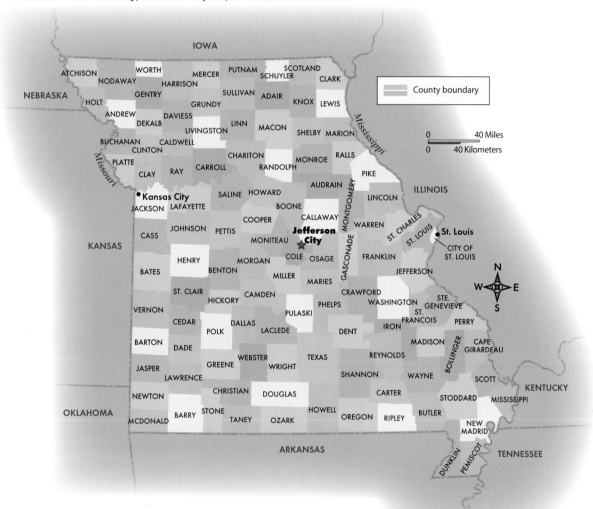

drawing in enough tax money to pay for county services. In 2007, some people were suggesting that Worth County should merge with another nearby county. On the other side of the state, some people are suggesting that the city of St. Louis merge with St. Louis County. They argue that the combined government would be better able to serve its citizens.

State Flag

The Missouri state flag has three horizontal stripes of red, white, and blue. The red stripe represents valor; the white stripe represents purity; and the blue stripe represents vigilance, permanency, and justice. The Missouri state seal appears in the center of the flag, signifying both Missouri's independence as a state and its place as a part of the whole United States. Having the state seal in the center of the national colors of red, white, and blue shows that Missouri is the geographical center of the nation. Twenty-four stars encircle the state seal, indicating that Missouri was the 24th state admitted to the Union. The flag, which was designed by Cape Girardeau resident Marie Oliver, was adopted in 1913.

State Seal

In the middle of the Missouri state seal is a shield. On the right side of the shield, a bald eagle grasps the olive branches of peace and the arrows of war in its talons. This represents the strength and powers of the federal government. On the left side of the shield are a grizzly bear and a crescent moon. The bear symbolizes the strength and bravery of Missourians. The moon symbolizes the possibility of a greater future. A belt inscribed with "United we stand, divided we fall" encircles the shield.

Two more grizzly bears are on opposite sides of the shield. They stand on a scroll inscribed with the state motto, *Salus populi suprema lex esto*, which is Latin for "Let the welfare of the people be the supreme law." Above the shield is a helmet, which symbol-izes that Missouri is a strong, independent state. Above this is a large star sur-rounded by 24 smaller stars, signifying that Missouri was the 24th state.

Robert Wells—a lawyer, state legisla-tor, and judge— designed the seal. It was adopted on January 11, 1822.

READ ABOUT

An engineer
outlines plans
at a Boeing
aircraft factory
in St. Louis.

ECONOMY ECONOMY ECONOMY ECONOMY ECONOMY ECONOMY ECONOMY

CHAPTER EIGHT

ECONOMY

★

M ISSOURI SITS AT THE CROSS-
ROADS OF THE NATION. Trucks,
trains, airplanes, and barges
head out from Missouri to points across the
country. Kansas City is the nation's third-
largest truck terminal. St. Louis is the nation's
second-largest inland port. These trucks and
trains carry factory goods and farm products
from one part of the country to another, but
manufacturing and agriculture no longer
dominate the Missouri economy. Instead,
services play the largest role.

100

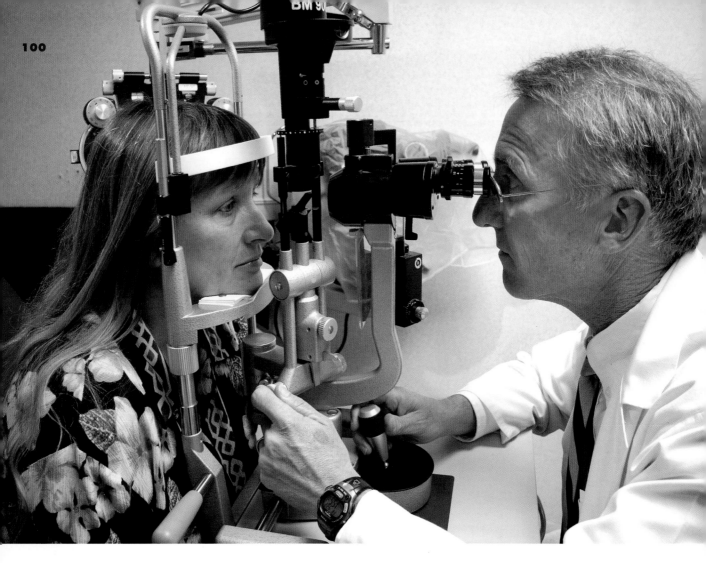

An ophthalmologist checks a patient's eyes at the Mason Eye Institute at the University of Missouri.

W★W

C. H. Laessig built the world's first gasoline station in St. Louis in 1905. His customers were able to fill their tanks through a garden hose rather than buying gasoline by the can.

SERVICE INDUSTRIES

The vast majority of Missourians work in service industries. They don't make or grow a product. Instead, they do work that helps others. Bank tellers, teachers, gas station attendants, bus drivers, and lawyers all work in service industries.

In Missouri, health care, education, and tourism are among the largest service industries. Millions of people visit Branson every year to enjoy live music in a beautiful setting. The finance and real estate industries are also important. H&R Block, the nation's leading tax preparation company, is headquartered in Kansas City.

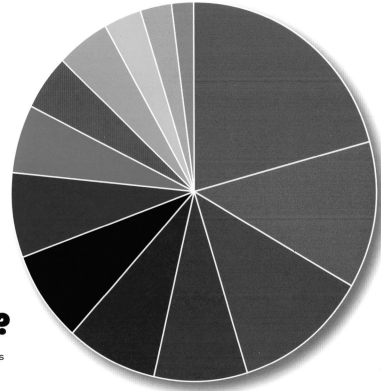

What Do Missourians Do?

This color-coded chart shows what industries Missourians work in.

21.0% Educational services, health care, and social assistance, 577,273

12.6% Manufacturing, 346,590

11.9% Retail trade, 326,637

8.2% Arts, entertainment, recreation, accommodation, and food services, 225,867

8.1% Professional, scientific, management, administrative, and waste management services, 224,403

7.7% Construction, 210,906

7.4% Finance, insurance, real estate, rental, and leasing, 201,777

5.6% Transportation, warehousing, and utilities, 152,646

4.9% Other services, except public administration, 133,989

4.6% Public administration, 125,053

3.5% Wholesale trade, 95,493

2.7% Information, 73,317

1.8% Agriculture, forestry, fishing, hunting, and mining, 49,980

Source: U.S. Census Bureau, 2005 estimate

MANUFACTURING

Manufacturing accounts for 15 percent of Missouri's economy. The state's major manufacturing products include chemicals and transportation equipment such as motor vehicles, railroad cars, and airplanes. Many Missouri products are exported to other countries. By far the largest category of exports is transportation equipment, such as engines and vehicle assembly. Most of the exports go to Canada.

Aunt Jemima Pancake Mix was the first ready-mix made for the public. Chris L. Rutt, a newspaper reporter in St. Joseph, invented it in 1889. He named it after a song that was popular at the time.

Missouri also makes many food products. Folgers Coffee has been roasting coffee in Kansas City since 1907. Now owned by Procter & Gamble, it still has a huge roasting facility in Kansas City that produces most of the company's coffee.

The nation's largest brewery, or beer-making business, is Anheuser-Busch, which is headquartered in St. Louis. Eberhard Anheuser, an immigrant from Germany, bought a small brewery in 1860. Four years later, his son-in-law, Adolphus Busch, joined him in the business. They were the first brewers to **pasteurize** beer to keep it fresh and the first to use refrigerated railway cars to transport their beer.

Monsanto Company doesn't produce food, but its work affects the food you eat. John Francis Queeny founded the company in 1901 in St. Louis. His first product was saccharin, an artificial sweetener. In recent years, the company has been altering the **genes** in seeds to improve crops. It also manufactures a substance that makes cows produce more milk. Monsanto is one of the nation's top 10 chemical companies.

In 1929, Charles L. Grigg of St. Louis invented the soft drink he called Bib-Label Lithiated Lemon-Lime Soda. He changed its name to the more catchy 7UP two years later.

MINI-BIO

JOYCE C. HALL: THE MAN WHO "CARED ENOUGH"

Joyce C. Hall (1891–1982) was a Nebraskan who moved to Kansas City as a teenager. Determined to start a business for himself, he arrived with shoe boxes full of postcards, which he sold door-to-door. After his brother joined him, they started a company that made greeting cards. In 1954, the Hall Brothers Company became Hallmark. Hall believed firmly in advertising. In the mid-20th century, it seemed that all Americans knew the company slogan, "When you care enough to send the very best." Hallmark, the world's largest greeting card company, is still headquartered in Kansas City.

❓ **Want to know more?** See www.nsea.org/news/HallProfile.htm

Major Agricultural and Mining Products

This map shows where Missouri's major agricultural and mining products come from. See a chicken? That's where poultry is raised.

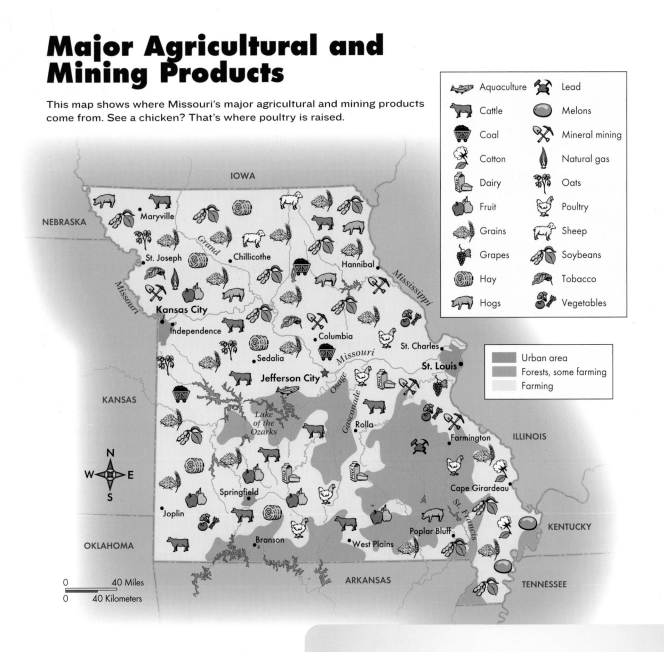

🐟	Aquaculture	🦀	Lead
🐄	Cattle	🥚	Melons
	Coal	⚒️	Mineral mining
	Cotton		Natural gas
	Dairy		Oats
	Fruit	🐔	Poultry
	Grains	🐑	Sheep
🍇	Grapes		Soybeans
	Hay		Tobacco
🐖	Hogs		Vegetables

	Urban area
	Forests, some farming
	Farming

Top Products

Manufacturing	Transportation equipment, processed foods, chemicals
Mining	Lead, crushed stone, lime
Agriculture	Soybeans, corn, cotton, wheat
Livestock	Cattle, hogs, dairy products, turkeys

Dairy cows grazing in a Missouri field

A pecan farm in Brunswick in north-central Missouri boasts the World's Largest Pecan. The giant concrete nut weighs about 12,000 pounds (5,400 kg).

WORD TO KNOW

equine *related to the horse family*

AGRICULTURE

Missouri is second only to Texas in its total number of farms—it has about 105,000 of them. The state's major crops are soybeans and corn. Most of the corn grown in Missouri is used to feed cattle. The state also produces hay, cotton, wheat, sorghum, apples, and pecans.

Livestock accounts for about one-third of Missouri's farm income. Though the Kansas City Stockyards closed in 1991, cattle remain the state's number-one livestock product. Most of the state's cattle are raised on the northern plains and the Osage Prairie. Missouri also produces large numbers of hogs, chickens, and turkeys.

Missouri ranks third in the nation in sales of **equine** animals. Hundreds of Missouri breeders sell all types of horses. One popular breed, the Missouri fox trotter, comes from the Ozarks. Pioneers found this strong horse useful on the rocky ground of the Ozarks.

When William Becknell established the Santa Fe Trail in 1821, he brought back some hardy Mexican mules and donkeys. Missouri farmers bred them into the famed Missouri mule. The Missouri mule is a cross between a female draft horse and a male donkey. Missouri was known around the world for the quality and quantity of its mules. Several Missouri companies still breed and sell mules. Trail riders in rough country sometimes prefer mules because they are more sure-footed than horses.

MINING

Missouri has long been the nation's top lead-producing state. Most of the state's lead mines are in or near the St. Francois Mountains. Zinc, iron, and copper are found in Missouri. The state's other important mining products include crushed stone, lime, and sand and gravel.

SEE IT HERE!

AN UNDERGROUND WORLD
The Hunt Midwest SubTropolis in north Kansas City is the world's largest underground storage facility. This 1,000-acre (400 hectare) site is located in a cave created by limestone mining. An additional 35 acres (14 ha) are added to the site every year as the mining continues. Companies rent space in the SubTropolis for use as offices and warehouses. Nearly 7 miles (11 km) of paved and lighted roads and 2 miles (3 km) of railroad tracks run through the facility, which has parking for 1,800 employees. The U.S. Postal Service is the facility's largest tenant.

Missouri mules transporting materials near the Panama Canal in 1940

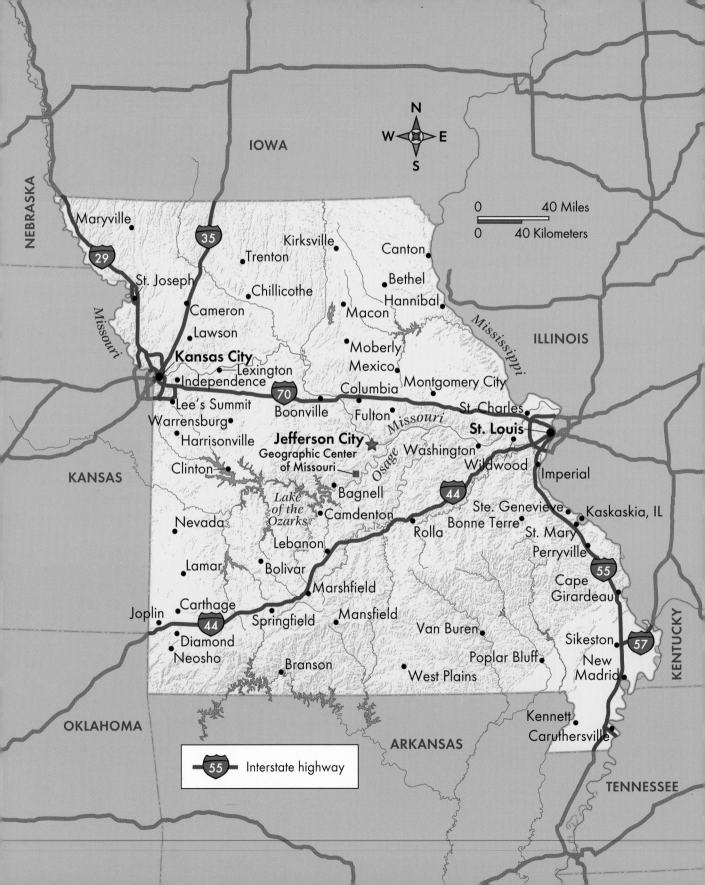

NEBRASKA

IOWA

N
W   E
S

Maryville

35

29

Kirksville

Canton

Trenton

Bethel

St. Joseph

Chillicothe

Hannibal

Cameron

Macon

ILLINOIS

Lawson

Moberly

Mississippi

Kansas City

Lexington

Mexico

Independence

Columbia

Montgomery City

70

Lee's Summit

Boonville

Fulton

St. Charles

Warrensburg

Missouri

St. Louis

Harrisonville

Jefferson City
Geographic Center
of Missouri

Washington

Wildwood

KANSAS

Clinton

Osage

Imperial

44

Bagnell

Ste. Genevieve

Lake
of the
Ozarks

Camdenton

Bonne Terre

Kaskaskia, IL

Nevada

Rolla

St. Mary

Lebanon

Perryville

Lamar

Bolivar

55

Marshfield

Cape
Girardeau

Joplin

Carthage

44

Mansfield

Springfield

Sikeston

57

Diamond

Van Buren

New
Madrid

Neosho

Poplar Bluff

Branson

West Plains

KENTUCKY

OKLAHOMA

ARKANSAS

Kennett

Caruthersville

TENNESSEE

0   40 Miles
0   40 Kilometers

55   Interstate highway

CHAPTER NINE

TRAVEL GUIDE

★

FROM THE LUSH FORESTS OF THE OZARKS TO THE COBBLESTONE STREETS OF OLD ST. LOUIS, THE STATE OF MISSOURI IS A GREAT PLACE TO EXPLORE. It's time to put on your walking shoes and visit some Indian mounds, see where Mark Twain grew up, and hear some jazz. There's no time to waste—grab your map and let's go!

← Follow along with this travel map. We'll begin in Canton and travel all the way around the state to Independence!

124

U.S. Events

1886

Apache leader Geronimo surrenders to the U.S. Army, ending the last major Native American rebellion against the expansion of the United States into the West.

1917-18

The United States engages in World War I.

1920

The Nineteenth Amendment to the U.S. Constitution grants women the right to vote.

1929

The stock market crashes, plunging the United States more deeply into the Great Depression.

1941-45

The United States engages in World War II.

1951-53

The United States engages in the Korean War.

1964-73

The United States engages in the Vietnam War.

1991

The United States and other nations engage in the brief Persian Gulf War against Iraq.

2001

Terrorists hijack four U.S. aircraft and crash them into the World Trade Center in New York City, the Pentagon in Arlington, Virginia, and a Pennsylvania field, killing thousands.

2003

The United States and coalition forces invade Iraq.

Missouri Events

1869

The Hannibal Bridge across the Missouri River is completed, bringing the railroad to Kansas City.

1873

Susan Blow opens the first public kindergarten in the United States in St. Louis.

1900

1904

St. Louis hosts the world's fair.

1920s

Kansas City becomes a thriving jazz center.

1931

The Lake of the Ozarks is created by Bagnell Dam.

1945

President Harry Truman orders atomic bombs dropped on two Japanese cities.

1958

Branson begins developing as a tourist center.

1968

William Clay is elected Missouri's first African American congressman.

1980

2000

Courts order that Missouri schools desegregate.

2006

St. Louis gains population for the first time in more than 50 years.

GLOSSARY

★　★　★

abolitionists people who worked to end slavery

archaeologist a person who studies the remains of past human societies

arsenal a place where weapons are made or stored

aviary a large walk-in enclosure where birds have room to fly

ceded gave up or granted

equine related to the horse family

fault a break in the rock deep in the earth along which earthquakes may occur

feminist holding the belief that women are the political, economic, and social equals of men

genes chemicals in plants and animals that determine the traits passed from one generation to the next

glaciers slow-moving masses of ice

guerrilla describing soldiers who don't belong to regular armies; they often use surprise attacks and other uncommon battle tactics

latitude the position of a place, measured in degrees north or south of the equator

levees ridges of land built up along a riverbank to prevent flooding

missionaries people who try to convert others to a religion

mosaics patterns or pictures formed from small pieces of colored tile, glass, or stone

pasteurize to heat a liquid in order to kill germs in it

plateau an elevated part of the earth with steep slopes

repealed withdrawn; canceled

sediment material eroded from rocks and deposited elsewhere by wind, water, or glaciers

sedimentary formed from clay, sand, and gravel that settled at the bottom of a body of water

segregated separated from others, according to race, class, ethnic group, religion, or other factors

temperance moderation, especially in drinking alcoholic beverages

till the gravel and soil left behind after a glacier retreats

transcontinental crossing an entire continent

STATE SONG

★ ★ ★

"Missouri Waltz"

State seal

"Missouri Waltz" became the state song on June 30, 1949. The origin of the song is unclear, although historians generally agree Frederick Knight Logan first printed it around 1912 after obtaining the melody from orchestra leader John Valentine Eppel. In 1914, the Forster Publishing Company bought the rights to the melody. Jim Shannon added lyrics. The song became popular when Harry Truman was president. He often played the tune on the White House piano.

Hush-a-bye, ma baby, slumbertime is comin' soon;
Rest yo' head upon my breast while Mommy hums a tune;
The sandman is callin' where shadows are fallin',
While the soft breezes sigh as in days long gone by.

Way down in Missouri where I heard this melody,
When I was a little child upon my Mommy's knee;
The old folks were hummin'; their banjoes were strummin';
So sweet and low.

Strum, strum, strum, strum, strum,
Seems I hear those banjoes playin' once again,
Hum, hum, hum, hum, hum,
That same old plaintive strain.

Hear that mournful melody,
It just haunts you the whole day long,
And you wander in dreams back to Dixie, it seems,
When you hear that old time song.

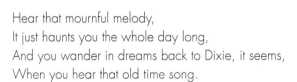

Hush-a-bye, ma baby, go to sleep on Mommy's knee,
Journey back to Dixieland in dreams again with me;
It seems like your Mommy is there once again,
And the old folks were strummin' that same old refrain.

Way down in Missouri where I learned this lullaby,
When the stars were blinkin' and the moon was climbin' high,
Seems I hear voices low, as in days long ago,
Singin' hush-a-bye.

NATURAL AREAS AND HISTORIC SITES

★ ★ ★

National Monument

Missouri is home to one national monument, the *George Washington Carver National Monument*, which features the hills, woodlands, and prairies surrounding the boyhood home of Carver, an African American botanist.

National Scenic Riverways

The *Ozark National Scenic Riverways* is the state's only national scenic riverway system. Visitors can canoe, swim, and fish in the clear waters of the Current and Jacks Fork rivers. They can also explore caves and bluffs and enjoy diverse plant and animal life.

National Expansion Memorial

The *Jefferson National Expansion Memorial* features the Gateway Arch, the Museum of Westward Expansion, and St. Louis's Old Courthouse, all in celebration of the spirit of the western pioneers.

National Battlefield

Wilson's Creek National Battlefield commemorates the first major battle of the Civil War fought west of the Mississippi River.

National Historic Sites

The *Harry S Truman National Historic Site* includes the home where the 33rd president lived from 1919 until his death and the family farm he worked on as a young man.

The *Ulysses S. Grant National Historic Site* features the house, barn, icehouse, and other buildings on the farm where Grant lived for part of his adult life. The site commemorates the 18th president's life, military career, and presidency.

National Historic Trails

Six national historic trails cross Missouri. They are the *California National Historic Trail;* the *Lewis & Clark National Historic Trail;* the *Oregon National Historic Trail;* the *Pony Express National Historic Trail;* the *Santa Fe National Historic Trail;* and the *Trail of Tears National Historic Trail.*

State Parks and Forests

Missouri's state park system features 83 state park and recreation areas, including *Big Lake State Park, Elephant Rocks State Park, Onondaga Cave State Park,* and *Route 66 State Park.*

Omar N. Bradley (1893–1981) was a U.S. Army general who led troops in North Africa and Europe during World War II. He later became the chairman of the Joint Chiefs of Staff, the principal military adviser to the president.

Martha Jane Cannary (Calamity Jane) See page 56.

Kit Carson (1809–1868) was a legendary guide in the American West. He also led military actions against the Navajo people, forcing them on a march across New Mexico. He was born in Franklin.

George Washington Carver See page 113.

Kate Chopin (1850–1904) wrote the early feminist novel *The Awakening.* She was born in St. Louis.

William Clark (1770–1838), along with Meriwether Lewis, led the expedition to explore the Louisiana Purchase. He later served as governor of the Missouri Territory.

Walter Cronkite

Walter Cronkite (1916–) was the anchorman of the *CBS Evening News* for 19 years. He was often called "the most trusted man in America" because of his vast journalistic experience and his serious yet kindly manner. He was born in St. Joseph.

Sheryl Crow (1962–) is a Grammy Award–winning rock singer, songwriter, and guitarist. She is a native of Kennett.

Walt Disney See page 80.

Thomas Stearns (T.S.) Eliot (1888–1965) was a pioneer of modern poetry whose works include *The Waste Land* and *"The Love Song of J. Alfred Prufrock."* Born in St. Louis, he was awarded the Nobel Prize in Literature.

Betty Grable (1916–1973) was a top movie star of the 1940s who appeared in films such as *Moon over Miami* and *Tin Pan Alley.* She was born in St. Louis.

Joyce C. Hall See page 102.

William Least Heat-Moon (1940–) is a travel writer who writes about small-town and rural America. His works include *Blue Highways* and *PrairyErth.* Part Osage, Irish, and English, he was born in Kansas City.

William Least Heat-Moon

Robert "Cal" Hubbard See page 87.

Edwin P. Hubble (1889–1953) was an astronomer who discovered that the universe is expanding. His ideas were used in developing the Big Bang theory of the origins of the universe. He was born in Marshfield.

Langston Hughes (1902–1967) was a poet, playwright, novelist, and newspaper columnist whose work explored African American life. He was born in Joplin.

Frank and Jesse James See page 54.

Scott Joplin See page 81.

Meriwether Lewis (1774–1809), with William Clark, led the expedition to explore the Louisiana Purchase. He later served as governor of the Louisiana Territory and lived in St. Louis.

Elijah P. Lovejoy (1802–1837) was the editor of a newspaper published in St. Louis. He was murdered for his abolitionist views.

Alexander McNair See page 45.

Marianne Moore (1887–1972) was a leading poet of the 20th century. Her *Collected Poems* of 1951 won the Pulitzer Prize and the National Book Award.

Stan Musial

Stan Musial (1920–) played for the St. Louis Cardinals for 22 years. He led the National League in batting average seven times in his career and was inducted into the Baseball Hall of Fame in 1969.

Carry Nation See page 62.

Nelly (Cornell Haynes Jr.) (1974–), who grew up in St. Louis, is one of the best-selling rap singers of all time. His hits include "Hot in Here" and "Dilemma."

Charlie Parker (1920–1955) was one of the most influential jazz saxophonists and composers of all time. He was instrumental in developing the bebop style of jazz, which features fast tempos, complex harmonies, and frequent improvisations. He grew up in Kansas City.

Thomas Pendergast See page 63.

Marlin Perkins (1905–1986) was a zoologist, the head of the St. Louis Zoo, and the host of the TV program *Wild Kingdom* from 1963 to 1984. He was born in Carthage.

John Pershing See page 61.

Langston Hughes

Brad Pitt (1963–) is one of the most popular actors in Hollywood. He has appeared in films such as *A River Runs Through It*, *Legends of the Fall*, and *Ocean's Eleven*. He grew up in Springfield.

Joseph Pulitzer (1847–1911) was the publisher of the *St. Louis Post-Dispatch*; he established the Pulitzer Prizes.

Nellie Tayloe Ross (1876–1977), a native of St. Joseph, was the first female governor in the nation's history. She became governor of Wyoming in 1925.

Charles M. Russell (1864–1926) was a painter and sculptor best known for his scenes of the American West. He was born in St. Louis.

Harry S Truman See page 93.

Mark Twain See page 83.

Brad Pitt

Laura Ingalls Wilder

Mona Van Duyn (1921–2004) was a poet who taught at Washington University in St. Louis for many years. She was the nation's first female poet laureate.

Mort Walker (1923–) is a cartoonist who created the comic strips *Beetle Bailey* and *Hi and Lois*. He was raised in Kansas City.

Laura Ingalls Wilder (1867–1957) moved with her pioneer family from Wisconsin to Minnesota, Iowa, and the Dakotas. As an adult, she settled in Mansfield, Missouri, where she worked as a newspaper columnist and wrote books about her childhood. These books, such as *Little House on the Prairie* and *On the Banks of Plum Creek*, have become classics of children's literature.

Tennessee Williams (1911–1983) was a playwright who wrote the classic dramas *A Streetcar Named Desire*, *The Glass Menagerie*, and *Cat on a Hot Tin Roof*. He spent much of his childhood in St. Louis.

RESOURCES

BOOKS

Nonfiction

Blashfield, Jean F. *The Oregon Trail*. Minneapolis: Compass Point Books, 2001.

Blashfield, Jean F. *The Santa Fe Trail*. Minneapolis: Compass Point Books, 2001.

Harness, Cheryl. *The Trailblazing Life of Daniel Boone and How Early Americans Took to the Road*. New York: Random House, 2007.

Lourie, Peter. *On the Trail of Lewis & Clark: A Journey up the Missouri River*. Honesdale, Pa.: Boyds Mills Press, 2004.

McPherson, James M. *Fields of Fury: The American Civil War*. New York: Atheneum, 2002.

Robinson, J. Dennis. *Jesse James: Legendary Rebel and Outlaw*. Minneapolis: Compass Point Books, 2006.

Swain, Gwenyth. *Dred and Harriet Scott: A Family's Struggle for Freedom*. St. Paul, Minn.: Borealis Books, 2004.

Wilder, Laura Ingalls. *On the Way Home: The Diary of a Trip from South Dakota to Mansfield, Missouri, in 1894*. New York: Harper & Row, 1962.

Fiction

Ambrose, Stephen. *This Vast Land: A Young Man's Journal of the Lewis and Clark Expedition*. New York: Simon & Schuster, 2003.

Jackson, Louise A. *Exiled: From Tragedy to Triumph on the Missouri Frontier*. Austin, Tex.: Eakin Press, 2007.

Twain, Mark. *The Adventures of Tom Sawyer*. New York: Penguin, 2006. First published 1876.

DVDs

Discoveries . . . America: Missouri. Bennett-Watt Entertainment, 2005.
Mark Twain. Florentine Films, 2001.
Meet Me in St. Louis. Metro-Goldwyn-Mayer, 1944.
Rivers of North America: Missouri River. Film Ideas, Inc., 2006.

WEB SITES AND ORGANIZATIONS

Harry S. Truman Library & Museum
www.trumanlibrary.org/kids/index.html
To learn more about Missouri's only native-born president.

Kansas City: A Wide Open Town
www.pbs.org/jazz/places/places_kansas_city.htm
To read all about Kansas City during its jazz heyday.

Missouri Kids!
www.sos.mo.gov/kids
For all kinds of information and activities about Missouri, from the secretary of state's office.

Missouri State Archives: All About Missouri History
www.sos.mo.gov/archives/history/
To learn more about the history of the state.

Missouri State Government
www.state.mo.us
To learn about the work of the Missouri government.

The Official Tourism Site for the State of Missouri
www.visitmo.com
Find out where to go and what to do in the Show-Me State.

INDEX

★ ★ ★

AUTHOR'S TIPS AND SOURCE NOTES

★ ★ ★

I used the resources at the Wisconsin State Historical Society while researching this book. It has one of the best book collections about North America available anywhere. Among the books I counted on was *Missouri: A Guide to the "Show Me" State*. This book was written during the Great Depression, when the federal government hired writers to produce a book about each state. Filled with historical and travel details, these books continue to be a valuable resource for writers today. *Missouri Then and Now*, by Perry McCandless and William E. Foley, was equally useful.

Of course, I used the Internet, too. Particularly helpful was the Missouri state archives site, www.sos.mo.gov/archives/history, where you can read about everything from the history of dueling in Missouri to the effects of the Dred Scott decision.